Modern
Standard
Arabic
Grammar

T0346506

Modern
Standard
Arabic
Grammar

A CONCISE GUIDE

قواعد العربية
الفصحى المعاصرة

Azza
Hassanein

The American University in Cairo Press
Cairo   New York

First published in 2006 by
The American University in Cairo Press
113 Sharia Kasr el Aini, Cairo, Egypt
420 Lexington Avenue, Suite 1644, New York, NY 10170
www.aucpress.com

Dar el Kutub No. 23749/05
ISBN 978 977 416 012 7

5 6 7 8 9   28 27 26 25 24

Designed by Fatiha Bouzidi

المحتويات
Contents

إهداء
Acknowledgments

I would like to thank my students, May Welsh, Lee Smith, Nour Aziza, Tiffany Bradley, Aisha Tray, and Sara Islam who first suggested that I put these notes into book form. The idea would not have occurred to me otherwise. I also would like to thank my students, Miller Sherling, James O'Keefe, Cameron Cross, and Timothy Quinn and colleagues, Hala Yehia, Mohamed Al Sharkawi, Laila El-Sawi, and Dalal Abo El-Seoud who read the book for evaluation and suggestions.

My gratitude and special thanks go to Mrs. Nariman Warraki, the director of the Arabic Language Institute (ALI), who supported me and my project even when it was just an abstract idea. Her continuous encouragement enabled me to go on with the project.

مقدمة
Introduction

This book is designed to be a grammar guide for students of Arabic as a foreign language. It does not introduce the grammar of Modern Standard Arabic (MSA) as such; nor does it claim to provide an overview of the language. It is a functional guide to the important rules of grammar as used in the curriculum of the Arabic Language Institute at the American University in Cairo. It focuses specifically on the grammar aspects of *al-Kitab al-Asasi*, albeit not in the same order. Students should consider this guide a study aid rather than a primary text.

The student will not find in this guide a battery of exercises or drills. It only presents rules in simple explanation. The guide, however, introduces a good number of examples and several tables for clarification.

Although the grammar points presented here correspond to *al-Kitab al-Asasi* in general, it deals with certain aspects as a whole rather than in separate parts. For example, verbs are dealt with as a group of related subjects, unlike in the book where verbs and conjugations are distributed throughout a number of chapters.

This guide is an accumulation of grammar handouts given to students over the course of several semesters. When it was collected in book form, it was given to a number of students and teachers for evaluation and recommendations. Their suggestions were discussed, and the book's current form is the final result of this process.

The book has been approved by a committee of teachers from the Arabic Language Institute.

الإشتقاقُ والميزانُ الصرفي
Derivation and the Pattern System

1. The majority of words in Arabic are derived from roots consisting of three radicals. Each root has a basic meaning that is shared by all words derived from that root.

2. Most words are formed by applying fixed patterns to the roots. Each pattern denotes a meaning. For example, the pattern فَاعِل denotes the meaning of the doer of a verb.

3. An Arabic word is derived by using a given root in a form dictated by one of the patterns. Accordingly, the meaning of that word reflects the meaning of the root as well as the meaning of the pattern. For example, the word كَاتِب carries the basic meaning of 'writing' from the root (ك ت ب), as well as the meaning of the pattern فَاعِل which signifies the doer of the verb, so that it means the one who writes (a writer).

4. In Arabic grammar, the three radicals of a root are symbolized by the letters ف, ع, ل. ف stands for the first radical, ع stands for the middle radical, and ل stands for the last radical.

5. The three radicals of a given word are symbolized by the letters of the
root plus the vowels of that word. For example:

كَتَبَ	is symbolized by	فَعَلَ
عَلِمَ	is symbolized by	فَعِلَ
عَظُمَ	is symbolized by	فَعُلَ

These فَعَلَ – فَعِلَ – فَعُلَ are called الأوزان (patterns).

6. In a given word, any letter (consonant or vowel) added to the three
radicals is to be added to the pattern. For example:

أرسل	is symbolized by	أفعل
تعلّم	is symbolized by	تفعّل
تعاون	is symbolized by	تفاعل

7. حروف الزيادة (letters of augmentation) are the letters that can be
added to the three radicals of the root to form different words. These
letters are:

أ - س - ت - ل - م - ن - ا - و - ي - هـ

2

أداة التعريف والحروف الشمسية والقمرية
The Definite Article and Solar and Lunar Letters

The Definite Article

1. The definite article in Arabic is (ال). It is basically equivalent to 'the' in English, but it is written as a part of the word (as a prefix).

2. The (ا) of the definite article may or may not be pronounced:

a. It is pronounced (أل) when it follows a pause (any interruption in speaking or reading). *'alkitaab* الكتاب

b. If it does not follow a pause, it is pronounced as a part of the preceding word and the 'a (أ) is elided in pronunciation only. For example:

فوق الكتاب *fawqal-kitaab*

3. If the preceding word ends in a long vowel, the long vowel must be shortened. In the pronunciation, *fii 'alkitaab* turns to *fil-kitaab* في الْكتاب.

4. The character of the first letter of a word to which the definite article is attached affects the pronunciation of (ل). Thus, it is pronounced before some consonants (lunar letters حروف قمرية) and elided before some others (solar letters حروف شمسية) which causes a doubling of the following consonant. For example:

'ashshams الشّمس – *'alqamar* القمر

Note: In writing, ال is always spelled the same regardless of how it is pronounced.

Solar and Lunar Letters

The words القمر (the moon), and الشّمس (the sun) are used to label the two groups of consonants mentioned above.

1. The solar letters are pronounced at, or near the same point of articulation as ل itself. They are:

ت - ث - د - ذ - ر - ز - س - ش - ص - ض - ط - ظ - ل - ن

2. The lunar letters are the rest, which are pronounced at a point in the mouth away from the ل. They are:

أ - ب - ج - ح - خ - ع - غ - ف - ق - ك - م - هـ - و - ي

أدوات الإستفهام
Interrogative Particles

مثال	معناها	الأداة
هل تدرس الألمانية؟ – نعم، أدرس الألمانية. – لا، لا أدرس الألمانية، بل أدرس العربية.	Interrogative, introducing direct and indirect question.	هل
أتدرس الألمانية؟ – نعم، أدرسها. – لا، لا أدرسها. ألن تدرس الألمانية؟ – بلى، سأدرسها. – نعم، لن أدرسها.	Like هل, but this particle is also used before negation.	(Prefix) أ
من أنت؟ – أنا طالب أدرس اللغة العربية.	Who	مَنْ
ما هذا؟ – هذا كتاب.	What	ما + اسم (a noun)
ماذا في الكتاب؟ – في الكتاب دروس مفيدة.		ماذا + حرف (a preposition)
ماذا تفعل؟ – أقرأ الكتاب.		ماذا + فعل (a verb)

متى زرت القاهرة؟ - زرتها العام الماضي.	When		متى
أين تدرس اللغة العربية؟ - أدرسها في الجامعة الأمريكية بالقاهرة.	Where		أين
كم طالبا في الفصل؟ - في الفصل عشرة طلاب.	How many (The noun after is singular, indefinite and in the accusative case)		كم
كيف حالك؟ - أنا بخير والحمد لله. كيف تذهب إلى الجامعة؟ - أذهب إلى الجامعة سيرا على الأقدام.	How		كيف
أي اللغات تدرس؟ - أدرس اللغة العربية.	Which, what		أي + اسم (إضافة)

General Notes:

١. All particles are indeclinable except (أي), which is declinable. (See explanation of these terms on page 8.) For example:

- أيُ نوع من الأصدقاء أنت؟
- أيَ لغة تدرس؟
- في أيِ فصل أنت؟

2. Sometimes, interrogative particles are preceded by a preposition. If the verb requires a preposition to be transitive, the preposition must come before the interrogative particle when forming a question.

- بماذا تكتب؟ أكتب بالقلم.
- إلى أين ستذهب؟ سأذهب إلى الجامعة.
- من أين أنت؟ أنا من مصر.
- بكم الكتاب؟ الكتاب بخمسين جنيها.

3. When the interrogative ما is preceded by a preposition, it may be written as one word with the preposition.

عن + ما ➡ عمَّ   في + ما ➡ فيمَ   إلى + ما ➡ إلامَ

4

الإعراب
Case

1. In Arabic, the endings of most words change depending on their grammatical functions in a specific sentence. This is called إعراب (case).

2. Arabic has four حالات إعرابية (case forms)
   a. الرفع   Nominative and indicative, for nouns and verbs.
   b. النصب   Accusative and subjunctive, for nouns and verbs.
   c. الجرّ   Genitive, for nouns only.
   d. الجزم   Jussive, for verbs only.

3. الإعراب is indicated by changes in words' endings, which is called علامات الإعراب. This change may be by short vowels (ضمة - فتحة - كسرة) or by suffixes. Words that are changeable are called كلمات معربة (declinable).

4. Some words have no distinctions of case. In other words, each word (noun or verb) has one form that does not change regardless of its grammatical function. These words are called كلمات مبنية (undeclinable). The indeclinable nouns do not take *tanween*. The indeclinable words are:

   a. Pronouns, such as: أنَا - هوَ - ـهـ
   b. Demonstratives, except dual forms, such as: هذَا - هؤلاء
   c. Relative pronouns, except dual forms, such as: الذي - الذينَ
   d. Interrogatives, except (أي), such as: كمْ - كيفَ - متَى
   e. Some adverbs. حيثُ - أمسِ - الآنَ - إذْ - إذَا - أينَ - ثمّ - هنَا- هناكَ

f. Numerals from 11-19, except 12. For example: أحدَ عشرَ - ثلاثةَ عشرَ

g. Perfect tense verbs. كتبَ - كتبُوا - كتبنَ

h. Plural feminine in imperfect tense verbs. هن يكتبنَ - أنتن تكتبنَ

i. Imperative. For example: اكتبْ (أنت) - اكتبَا (أنتما)

j. All prepositions and particles. For example: على - في - ثمّ - إنّ

5. Case endings of verbs will be demonstrated later (with verbs).

6. The following table shows the different علامات الإعراب (case endings) which represent the three الحالات الإعرابية (case forms) of nouns.

علامات إعراب الاسم   Case Endings of Nouns

الجمع *Plural*		المثنى *Dual*		المفرد *Singular*		الحالة الإعرابية
masc. مذكر	*fem.* مؤنث	*masc.* مذكر	*fem.* مؤنث	*masc.* مذكر	*fem.* مؤنث	
واو ـُونَ	ضمة ـاتُ	ألف ـانِ	ألف ـانِ	ضمّة ـُ	ضمّة ـُ	الرفع
ياء ـِينَ	كسرة ـاتِ	ياء ـَيْنِ	ياء ـَيْنِ	فتحة ـَ	فتحة ـَ	النصب
ياء ـِينَ	كسرة ـاتِ	ياء ـَيْنِ	ياء ـَيْنِ	كسرة ـِ	كسرة ـِ	الجر

7. The following table shows the different grammatical functions (الوظائف الإعرابية) of the three case forms.

الأسماء المجرورة	الأسماء المنصوبة	الأسماء المرفوعة
▪ المجرور بحرف جر	▪ خبر كان	▪ المبتدأ
▪ المضاف إليه	▪ اسم إن	▪ الخبر
▪ التابع للاسم المجرور (الصفة - المعطوف - التوكيد - البدل)	▪ المفعول به	▪ اسم كان
	▪ المفعول المطلق	▪ خبر إن
	▪ المفعول لأجله	▪ الفاعل
	▪ المفعول فيه (ظرف الزمان - ظرف المكان)	▪ نائب الفاعل
	▪ الحال	▪ التابع للاسم المرفوع (الصفة - المعطوف - التوكيد - البدل)
	▪ التمييز	
	▪ المنادى	
	▪ المستثنى	
	▪ المفعول معه	
	▪ التابع للاسم المنصوب (الصفة - المعطوف - التوكيد - البدل)	

5

المفرد والمثنى والجمع
Singular, Dual, and Plural

Arabic has three numbers: المفرد (singular) refers to one object, المثنى (dual) refers to two objects, and الجمع (plural) refers to three or more.

المثنى
Dual

Dual nouns are formed by adding the following suffixes to singular forms:
1. ـَان for the nominative case (مدرسَان) حالة الرفع
2. ـَيْن for the accusative and genitive (مدرسَيْن) حالتا النصب والجر

الجمع
Plural

There are two types of plural in Arabic:

أولاً: الجمع السالم First: Sound plural
The sound plural is formed by adding special suffixes to the singular form according to gender and case.

1. Masculine sound plural جمع المذكر السالم:
   a. ـُونَ for the nominative case (مدرسُونَ) حالة الرفع
   b. ـِينَ for the accusative and genitive (مدرسِينَ) حالتا النصب والجر

2. Feminine sound plural جمع المؤنث السالم:

   a. ـَاتُ for the nominative case (مدرسَاتُ) حالة الرفع

   b. ـَاتِ for the accusative and genitive (مدرسَاتِ) حالتا النصب والجر

Note: Dual and masculine sound plurals do not have تنوين, while feminine sound plurals and broken plurals do when necessary.

ثانياً: جمع التكسير Second: Broken plural

The broken plural is formed by internal changes to the singular form. So, the pattern of a broken plural may be different from its singular. For example:

شبّاك - (ج) شبابيك

In some cases, it is possible to predict the form of a broken plural, but it is better to learn broken plurals together with the corresponding singular forms.

Like singular words, the case of the broken plural may be indicated by كسرة - ضمة - فتحة, and it may take تنوين. Examples:

كتاب - (ج) كتب
طالب - (ج) طلاب
فصل - (ج) فصول

Some broken plurals:

school	مدارس	مدرسة	.1
institute	معاهد	معهد	.2
classroom	فصول	فصل	.3
lesson	دروس	درس	.4
pencil	أقلام	قلم	.5
office / desk	مكاتب	مكتب	.6
book	كتب	كتاب	.7
door	أبواب	باب	.8
window	شبابيك	شبّاك	.9
room	غرف	غرفة	.10
professor / Mr.	أساتذة	أستاذ	.11
student	طلاب	طالب	.12
friend	أصدقاء	صديق	.13
title / address	عناوين	عنوان	.14
job	وظائف	وظيفة	.15
person	أشخاص	شخص	.16
people	ناس	إنسان	.17
child	أطفال	طفل	.18
boy	أولاد	ولد	.19
girl	بنات	بنت	.20
man	رجال	رجل	.21
woman	نساء	امرأة	.22
country	بلاد	بلد	.23
city	مدن	مدينة	.24
country	دول	دولة	.25
house	بيوت	بيت	.26
street	شوارع	شارع	.27

6

أَسْماء الإِشارة
Demonstratives

المؤنث البعيد	المؤنث القريب	المذكر البعيد	المذكر القريب	
تِلْكَ	هَذِهِ	ذَاكَ - ذَلِكَ	هَذَا	المفرد
	هَاتَانِ (رفع) هَاتَيْنِ (نصب - جر)		هَذَانِ (رفع) هَذَيْنِ (نصب - جر)	المثنى
أُولَئِكَ	هَؤُلَاءِ	أُولَئِكَ	هَؤُلَاءِ	الجمع

1. أسماء الإشارة are indeclinable nouns (أسماء مبنية) except the dual forms as indicated in the table above.

2. اسم الإشارة agrees with the noun it refers to in gender and number, and if dual, case agreement is required as well. Examples:

هذا الرجل مجتهد. — هذه السيدة مجتهدة.

هذان الطالبان مجتهدان. — قابلت هذين الطالبين.

3. The noun which follows اسم الإشارة is always definite. For example:

هذا الكتاب مفيد (This book is useful.)

Otherwise the demonstrative and the noun it refers to form a sentence. For example:

هذا كتاب. (This is a book.)

4. The noun after اسم الإشارة takes the same case as the demonstrative. For example:

هذا الكتابُ مفيد. — قرأت هذا الكتابَ. — الدرس في هذا الكتابِ.

5. If the demonstrative refers to an *idaafa* construction, it must follow the *idaafa*. For example:

(This student's book.) كتاب الطالب هذا.

7

صفة النسب

Nasab Adjectives

In order to form an adjective from a noun the suffix *iyy* (ـيّ) is attached to the noun. Adjectives formed with this suffix are called '*Nasab* Adjectives' صفة النسب. For example:

مؤنث	مذكر		
مصريّة	مصريّ	مصر	١.
لبنانيّة	لبنانيّ	لبنان	٢.
تونسيّة	تونسيّ	تونس	٣.
خشبيّة	خشبيّ	خشب	٤.
حديديّة	حديديّ	حديد	٥.

The following modifications are to be done before attaching the suffix:

1. The definite article, if present, must be omitted. For example:

مؤنث	مذكر		
عراقيّة	عراقيّ	العراق	١.
يابانيّة	يابانيّ	اليابان	٢.
صينيّة	صينيّ	الصين	٣.
سويديّة	سويديّ	السويد	٤.
هنديّة	هنديّ	الهند	٥.

Note: The definite article can be added later according to the context.

2. The final long vowel الـمـد , if present, must be omitted. For example:

مؤنث	مذكر		
أمريكيّة	أمريكيّ	أمريكا	.1
كنديّة	كنديّ	كندا	.2
بلجيكيّة	بلجيكيّ	بلجيكا	.3
فرنسيّة	فرنسيّ	فرنسا	.4
هولنديّة	هولنديّ	هولندا	.5

3. The final *yaa* (ـيا), if present, must be omitted. For example:

مؤنث	مذكر		
ليبيّة	ليبيّ	ليبيا	.1
سوريّة	سوريّ	سوريا	.2
بريطانيّة	بريطانيّ	بريطانيا	.3
أستراليّة	أستراليّ	أستراليا	.4
ألمانيّة	ألمانيّ	ألمانيا	.5

4. The feminine suffix *ta' marbuta* (ـة), if attached to the noun, must be omitted from the adjective. For example:

مؤنث	مذكر		
سعوديّة	سعوديّ	السعودية	.1
سياسيّة	سياسيّ	السياسة	.2

8

الإضافـة
Idaafa Construction

The word إضافة means 'addition' or 'annexion.' الإضافة is a unit consisting of two nouns where the first belongs to or is possessed by the second.

The first term of *idaafa* is called *mudaaf* (مضاف) and the second is called *mudaaf ilaih* مضاف إليه. (المضاف) is the possessed and مضاف إليه is the possessor.

The *idaafa* construction usually corresponds to one of three English constructions. They are:

1. The 'of' construction: The office of the employee مكتب الموظّف
2. The possessive ('s): The student's book كتاب الطالب
3. Constructions like: The school bus أتوبيس المدرسة

Important Notes:

1. The whole construction functions as a single unit in a sentence. It can be the subject or the object in a sentence. For example:

قابل الطالب مدرسَ الفصلِ.
قرأ مدرسُ الفصلِ المفردات.

2. The first term المضاف never takes the definite article nor is it definite by any other means, such as by being a pronoun.

3. The first term المضاف may be in any case according to its position in the sentence, while the second term المضاف إليه is always genitive.

a. Nominative مرفوع: .هذا هو كِتابُ الطالبِ
b. Accusative منصوب: .يتعلم الطلاب كِتابةَ الرسائلِ
c. Genitive مجرور: .ذهبت لمقابلة مديرِ الجامعةِ

4. The second term المضاف إليه determines the definiteness of the whole construction. For example:

كتاب طالب (a student's book) - كتاب الطالب (the student's book)

5. The *idaafa* construction may be composed of more than two words. In this case the last noun may only be definite. كتاب طالبِ الجامعةِ (the university student's book). The first word in the longer construction may be any case while all other terms are genitive.

6. If the first term المضاف is a dual or a plural noun ending with *nun* ن, the ن should be dropped. For example:

مدرسان + الجامعة ➡ مدرسا الجامعة

مدرسون + الجامعة ➡ مدرسو الجامعة

9

الضمائر المنفصلة والمتصلة

Pronouns: Separate Pronouns and Pronominal Suffixes

الضمائر المنفصلة
Separate Pronouns

الغائب (Third person)		ضمائر المخاطب (Second person)		ضمائر المتكلم (First person)	
(He)	هُوَ	(You *masc. sing.*)	أَنْتَ	(I)	أَنَا
(She)	هِيَ	(You *fem. sing.*)	أَنْتِ	(We)	نَحْنُ
(They *dual*)	هُمَا	(You *dual*)	أَنْتُمَا		
(They *masc. pl.*)	هُمْ	(You *masc. pl.*)	أَنْتُمْ		
(They *fem. pl.*)	هُنَّ	(You *fem. pl.*)	أَنْتُنَّ		

الضمائر المتصلة
Pronominal Suffixes

---

1. الضمائر المتصلة (attached pronouns) are suffixes attached to the ends of words. They may be attached to most parts of speech: Nouns, verbs, prepositions, etc. with different meanings resulting in each case.

2. When attached to nouns, they express possession. A pronominal suffix with a noun form an *idaafa* construction. For example: كتابه (his book).

3. When attached to verbs, they function as direct objects. For example:

قرأ الطالب الكتاب . ← قرأه .

4. The case endings of nouns do not change when pronominal suffixes are added. For example: هذا كتابه . — في كتابه .

The only exception is the first person singular suffix ي, which is attached directly to the noun without the case ending.

كتاب + أنا becomes كتابي in all cases.

5. There is a pronominal suffix corresponding to each of the independent pronouns.

The following table shows the different forms of pronominal suffixes:

متصل باسم *Attached to a Noun*		الضمير المتصل *Pronominal suffix*	الضمير المنفصل *Separate Pronoun*
my book	كتابي	ـي	أنا
our book	كتابنا	ـنَا	نحن
his book	كتابه	ـهُ	هو
her book	كتابها	ـهَا	هي
their *dual* book	كتابهما	ـهُمَا	هما
their *masc. pl.* book	كتابهم	ـهُمْ	هم
their *fem. pl.* book	كتابهن	ـهُنَّ	هنّ
your *masc. sing.* book	كتابك	ـكَ	أنت
your *fem. sing.* book	كتابك	ـكِ	أنت
your *dual* book	كتابكما	ـكُمَا	أنتما
your *masc. pl.* book	كتابكم	ـكُم	أنتم
your *fem. pl.* book	كتابكن	ـكُنَّ	أنتن

حروف الجر والاسم المجرور
Prepositions

Prepositions are indeclinable particles that place the noun after them in the genitive case. They are:

مِنْ - إِلَى - عَلَى - عَنْ - فِي - حَتَّى - كَـ - بِـ - لِـ - مُنْذُ - مُذْ - وَ (القسم Jurative) - تَـ (القسم)

Nouns after these prepositions are always in the genitive case. Examples:

الكتاب على المكتبِ. — ذاكرت حتى المساءِ.

حضرت منذ ساعةٍ. — واللهِ إن الصدق لمنجٍ.

Note: (و - تَـ القسم) are used before a noun, usually the name of God, when making an oath.

التوابع
Followers

1. التابع is a noun that agrees with the noun preceding it in case.

2. There are four types of التوابع, they are:
   a. Adjective الصفة.
   b. Coupling العطف.
   c. Substitution البدل.
   d. Emphasis التوكيد – التأكيد.

الصفة والموصوف
Noun-adjective

1. In Arabic, the adjective follows the noun it modifies. الجامعة الأمريكية

2. The adjective must agree with the noun it modifies in the following:

- Gender:	الطالب الأمريكي	الطالبة الأمريكية
- Number:	طالبان أمريكيان	طالب أمريكي
- Definiteness:	الطالب الأمريكي	طالب أمريكي
- Case:	قابلت الطالبَ الأمريكيَّ.	هذا هو الطالبُ الأمريكيُّ.

3. Note the difference between the following examples:
   a. الطالب الأمريكي (the American student): This is a noun-adjective phrase where the adjective agrees with the noun it modifies in gender, number, case, and definiteness.

b. إِنَّ الطالبَ أمريكِّي (the student is American): This is a complete nominal sentence introduced by إِنَّ, where اسم إِنَّ (الطالب) is accusative and definite, and خبر إِنَّ (أمريكي) is nominative and indefinite. The required agreement in this case is number agreement only.

العطف
Coupling

1.   العطف means that two words, phrases, or sentences are connected by a conjunction.

2.   The conjunctions حروف العطف are:

a.   و: means 'and' and connects two items of the same level.

حضر محمد وعلي.

b.   فـ: implies immediate succession of action.

حضر محمد فعلي. (علي حضر بعد محمد مباشرة)

c.   ثمَ: implies succession with an interval.

حضر محمد ثم علي. (علي حضر بعد محمد ببعض الوقت)

d.   أو: is used for choosing between alternatives.

سأدرس اللغة العربية في القاهرة أو دمشق.

e.   أم: means أو, but it is used in direct or indirect questions, and in certain constructions.

هل ستدرس العربية في القاهرة أم دمشق؟
لا أعرف هل أدرس العربية في القاهرة أم دمشق.
سأدرس العربية سواء في القاهرة أم دمشق.

f. سأدرس العربية لا الألمانية .is used for negation :لا

g. لن أدرس الألمانية لكن العربية .is used to rectify :لكن

h. لن أدرس الألمانية بل العربية .لكن is used like :بل

i. لم يحضر أحد إلى الفصل حتى المدرس ."means "even :حتى

البدل
Substitution
_____

1. This is a noun that indicates the noun it follows or part of it.
2. It has three types, but the most common type is: الأستاذ أحمد

التوكيد
Emphasis
_____

1. التوكيد is a noun which is placed after another noun to emphasize it.

2. The nouns that are used for التوكيد are:
كل - جميع - نفس - عين - عامة - كلا وكلتا (للمثنى)

3. The most commonly used are: كل - جميع - كلا وكلتا.
حضر الطلاب كلهم. حضر الطالبان كلاهما.

4. In order to consider those nouns توكيد, they must follow the noun they emphasize and must be attached to a pronoun referring to that noun.

أنواع الجملة العربية
Types of Sentences

There are two types of sentences in Arabic:

أولاً: الجملة الاسمية
First: The Nominal Sentence

1. الجملة الاسمية begins with a noun and consists of two main parts:
   a. مبتدأ (subject of a nominal sentence).
   b. خبر (predicate).

   أحمد طالب. (Ahmed is a student.)

2. الخبر may identify المبتدأ or describe it.

3. المبتدأ must be definite معرفة in order to start the sentence. It can be:
   a. a definite noun. الطالبُ مجتهدٌ
   b. a proper noun. محمدُ طالبٌ
   c. a pronoun. أنا طالبٌ
   d. a demonstrative. هذا طالبٌ
   e. a definite *idaafa* construction. كتابُ الطالبِ على المكتبِ

4. When المبتدأ is indefinite نكرة and الخبر is a prepositional or adverbial phrase شبه جملة, the usual order is الخبر first followed by المبتدأ. For example:

   في الفصلِ طالبٌ. (A student is in the classroom.)

5. الخبر may be:

    a. an indefinite noun. الطالبُ مجتهدٌ

    b. an adverbial phrase. الكتابُ فوقَ المكتبِ

    c. a prepositional phrase. الطالبُ في الفصلِ

    d. a nominal sentence. الطالبُ اسمُه أَحمدُ

    e. a verbal sentence. الطالبُ يكتب الدرسَ

    f. an *idaafa* construction. الطالبُ صديقُ المدرسِ

6. الجملة is considered اسمية when it begins with a noun even when الخبر is a verb. For example:

الطالبُ يكتب الدرسَ.

7. Both subject and predicate may be followed by an adjective(s) صفة. Examples:

الطالبُ الأمريكيُ الطويلُ يدرس اللغة العربية.
أحمد طالبٌ مجتهدٌ نشيطٌ.

8. Both subject and predicate are always in the nominative case مرفوع.

9. If الخبر is definite, a pronoun has to be used before it. This pronoun agrees with الخبر in gender and number. Examples:

هذا هو الكتابُ.
هذه هي القصةُ.
هذان هما الطالبَانِ.

ثانياً: الجملة الفعلية

Second: The Verbal Sentence

The Verbal Sentence الجملة الفعلية begins with a verb and consists of three
main parts:

- a. فعل (verb).
- b. فاعل (doer of the verb).
- c. مفعول به (object).

General notes:

1. The usual order of a verbal sentence is:

مفعول به	فاعل	فعل
الدرسَ	الطالبُ	كتبَ

2. The verb has to agree يطابق with the subject according to the rules of
verb-subject agreement. Examples:

يكتب الطالبُ. — تكتب الطالبةُ.

3. الفاعل is the doer of the action denoted by the verb, and is in the
nominative case مرفوع.

4. الفاعل may or may not be expressed in the sentence since it can be
indicated by the form of the verb. For example:

كَتَبَتْ الدرسَ. (She wrote the lesson.)

5. A verbal sentence may or may not contain an object مفعول به.
Examples:

نجحَ الطالبُ. — كتبَ الطالبُ الدرسَ.

6. The object المفعول به is in the accusative case منصوب.

7. In its simplest form, a verbal sentence consists of only one word. The subject can be indicated by the form of the verb and the object can be prefixed by a pronominal suffix. For example:

كَتَبَاهُ. (They *dual masculine* wrote it.)

8. The subject and the object may be modified by one or more adjectives. For example:

دخل الطالبُ الأمريكيُّ الفصلَ الجديدَ.

(The American student entered the new classroom.)

9. The verbal sentence may contain one or more adverbial or prepositional phrases modifying the verb. For example:

حضر الطالب من أمريكا قبل أسبوع.

الفِعـل
Verbs

Verbs الأفعال, as words, follow the derivational strategy نظام الاشتقاق. From each root, a definite group of verb patterns أوزان are formed. The pattern فعـل is considered the basic pattern where the letter ف stands for the first radical, ع stands for the second, and ل stands for the third.

From the basic pattern fourteen possible patterns are derived to express various modifications of the idea expressed by the basic one. The fourteen derived verb patterns plus the basic one constitute a total of fifteen patterns, only ten of which are used widely. They are:

I	يَفْعلُ	فَعلَ
II	يُفَعِّلُ	فَعَّلَ
III	يُفَاعِلُ	فَاعَلَ
IV	يُفْعِلُ	أَفْعَلَ
V	يَتَفَعَّلُ	تَفَعَّلَ
VI	يَتَفَاعَلُ	تَفَاعَلَ
VII	يَنْفَعِلُ	انْفَعَلَ
VII	يَفْتَعِلُ	افْتَعَلَ
IX	يَفْعَلُّ	افْعَلَّ
X	يَسْتَفْعِلُ	اسْتَفْعَلَ

These verbal derivatives المشتقات الفعلية share a general meaning derived from the basic meaning of the root, plus an extra meaning derived from the pattern itself.

The third masculine singular form of the perfect tense, which literally means 'he did/he does' فعل / يفعل, is used to list verbs in dictionaries instead of the infinitive in English.

زمن الفعل
Verb Tenses

The Arabic verb has the following tenses:

1. **Perfect** ماض: indicates completed events or actions.

2. **Imperfect** مضارع: indicates actions or events which have not been completed.

3. **The future tense** المستقبل: is expressed by the use of the particle سوف before the imperfect form, or by the prefix ـس.

شكل الفعل
Verb Form

The verb form consists of:

1. A stem, which is derived as mentioned above and denotes the meaning of the verb. There are three stem forms of verbs: perfect tense form الفعل الماضي , imperfect tense form الفعل المضارع, and imperative فعل الأمر which is used for giving a positive command or request (لا + الفعل المضارع المجزوم is used for negative commands).

2. The subject marker, in the form of affixes, indicates the person, gender, and number. Thus, it is not necessary to express a pronoun subject since the verb form includes a subject marker. كتب (he wrote) - يكتبون (they, *masculine*, write.)

تصريف الأفعال مع الضمائر
Verb Conjugation

Verbs in Arabic must be conjugated in order to agree with the subjects they refer to تتطابق مع الفَاعِل in gender الجنس and/or number العدد depending on the word order.

١. In a verbal sentence الجملة الفعلية, the order is always the verb الفعل first and then the subject الفاعل. In this case only gender agreement is required and the verb is always singular مفرد regardless of the number of the subject. Examples:

حضر المدرس.
حضر المدرسون.
حضرت المدرسات.

٢. When the subject الفاعل precedes the verb الفعل, both gender and number agreement تطابق الجنس والعدد are necessary. Number agreement is also required when the verb refers to a dual or plural subject which is mentioned in a previous sentence or is clear from the context. Examples:

درس الطلاب، وفهموا.
دخل الطالبان، وجلسا.

أنواع الفعل من حيث البنية
Verb Types

Verbs are divided into two types based on the nature of their radicals:

١. Strong Verbs الأفعال الصحيحة:
   a. Sound verb الفعل السالم: the three radicals are consonants, (أ) is not

one of the radicals, and the final consonant is not doubled.

كتب / يكتب - استقبل / يستقبل

b. الفعل المهموز: the first radical is (أ). أكل / يأكل - أخذ / يأخذ

c. Doubled verb الفعل المضعّف: the second and third radicals are identical. عدّ / يعدّ - استقرّ / يستقرّ

2. Weak Verbs الأفعال المعتلة:
   a. المعتل الأول: the first radical is a weak letter. وصل / يصل
   b. المعتل الوسط: the middle radical is a weak letter. قال / يقول
   c. المعتل الآخر: the third radical is a weak letter. استغنى / يستغني

قاعدة السكون

The *Sukun* (°) Rule:

If the *sukun* is a part of the form:

1. When conjugating the last two types of weak verbs, المعتل الوسط والمعتل الآخر, drop the weak letter when it is followed by a *sukun*.

2. Untie the doubled consonants when it is followed by a *sukun* (°).

The following table shows the pattern of verb conjugation that should be followed when conjugating any verb type.

If you memorize this table by heart along with some few general rules of Arabic, like the *sukun* rule, you will find it easy to conjugate all types and forms of verbs with different pronouns.

الأمر	المضارع	الماضي	الضمائر
فَعَلَ / يَفْعَلُ (to do)			

الأمر	المضارع	الماضي	الضمائر
	أَفْعَلُ	فَعَلْتُ	أنا
	نَفْعَلُ	فَعَلْنَا	نحن
اِفْعَلْ	تَفْعَلُ	فَعَلْتَ	أنتَ
اِفْعَلي	تَفْعَلِينَ	فَعَلْتِ	أنتِ
اِفْعَلَا	تَفْعَلَانِ	فَعَلْتُمَا	أنتما
اِفْعَلُوا	تَفْعَلُونَ	فَعَلْتُمْ	أنتم
اِفْعَلْنَ	تَفْعَلْنَ	فَعَلْتُنَّ	أنتنّ
	يَفْعَلُ	فَعَلَ	هو
	تَفْعَلُ	فَعَلَتْ	هي
	يَفْعَلَانِ	فَعَلَا	هما (masc.)
	تَفْعَلَانِ	فَعَلَتَا	هما (fem.)
	يَفْعَلُونَ	فَعَلُوا	هم
	يَفْعَلْنَ	فَعَلْنَ	هنّ

The Imperative (الأمر) is Formed from the Second Person Imperfect as Follows:

1. Remove the subject marker (the prefix).

2. Put it in the jussive mood (الجزم) by:
   a. replacing the final vowel (ُ) with (ْ) when using the verb with أنتَ.

b. dropping the final (ن) with أنتِ – أنتما – أنتم.

c. no change occurs with أنتنَ.

3. When the vowel of the first radical (after removing the subject marker) is a *sukun* (ْ), add (١) because Arabic words can not start with a *sukun*.

4. The added (١) takes a *damma* (ُ) if the middle radical of the present tense of the verb takes (ُ), and a *kasra* (ِ) if the middle radical takes a *kasra* (ِ) or a *fatha* (َ). Examples:

كَتَبَ / يَكْتُبُ / أُكْتُبْ — جَلَسَ / يَجْلِسُ / اِجْلِس — فَتَحَ / يَفْتَحُ / اِفْتَحْ

5. When the first radical is a *hamza* (أ) and the verb is form I, remove the *hamza*. For example:

أَكَلَ / يَأْكُلُ / كُلْ

The conjugation of different verb types with different pronouns in different tenses is the subject of the next chapter.

14

تصريف الأفعال المختلفة مع الضمائر
Verb Conjugations

تصريف الفعل السالم مع الضمائر المختلفة
Sound Verb Conjugation

Form I: All forms of this type are conjugated the same. Here is an example:

الأمر	المضارع	الماضي	الضمائر
			كَتَبَ / يَكْتُبُ *(to write)*
	أَكْتُبُ	كَتَبْتُ	أنا
	نَكْتُبُ	كَتَبْنَا	نحن
اُكْتُبْ	تَكْتُبُ	كَتَبْتَ	أنتَ
اُكْتُبِي	تَكْتُبِينَ	كَتَبْتِ	أنتِ
اُكْتُبَا	تَكْتُبَانِ	كَتَبْتُمَا	أنتما
اُكْتُبُوا	تَكْتُبُونَ	كَتَبْتُم	أنتم
اُكْتُبْنَ	تَكْتُبْنَ	كَتَبْتُنَّ	أنتنّ
	يَكْتُبُ	كَتَبَ	هو
	تَكْتُبُ	كَتَبَتْ	هي
	يَكْتُبَانِ	كَتَبَا	هما *(masc.)*
	تَكْتُبَانِ	كَتَبَتَا	هما *(fem.)*
	يَكْتُبُونَ	كَتَبُوا	هم
	يَكْتُبْنَ	كَتَبْنَ	هنّ

Other Forms: All other forms are conjugated the same as form I.

Doubled Verb Conjugation

Form I: The following table shows the conjugation with different pronouns in different tenses. Note that the doubled consonant is untied when it is followed by a *sukun*.

الأمر	المضارع	الماضى	الضمير
عَدَّ / يَعُدُّ (*to count*)			
	أَعُدُّ	عَدَدْتُ	أنا
	نَعُدُّ	عَدَدْنَا	نحن
عُدَّ	تَعُدُّ	عَدَدْتَ	أنتَ
عُدِّي	تَعُدِّينَ	عَدَدْتِ	أنتِ
عُدَّا	تَعُدَّان	عددْتُمَا	أنتما
عُدُّوا	تَعُدُّونَ	عَدَدْتم	أنتم
اُعْدُدْنَ	تَعْدُدْنَ	عَدَدْتُنَّ	أنتنّ
	يَعُدُّ	عَدَّ	هو
	تَعُدُّ	عَدَّتْ	هي
	يَعُدَّان	عَدَّا	هما (*masc.*)
	تَعُدَّان	عَدَّتا	هما (*fem.*)
	يَعُدُّونَ	عَدُّوا	هم
	يَعْدُدْنَ	عَدَدْنَ	هنّ

Other Forms: All other forms are conjugated the same as form I.

Sound Verb (with *hamza* as first radical) Conjugation

Form I: These verbs are conjugated the same as sound verbs, except that the *hamza* is dropped when forming the imperative.

الأمر	المضارع	الماضي	الضمير
		أَكَلَ / يَأْكُلُ *(to eat)*	
	آكُلُ	أَكَلْتُ	أنا
	نَأْكُلُ	أَكَلْنَا	نحن
كُلْ	تَأْكُلُ	أَكَلْتَ	أنتَ
كُلِي	تَأْكُلِينَ	أَكَلْتِ	أنتِ
كُلَا	تَأْكُلَانِ	أَكَلْتُمَا	أنتما
كُلُوا	تَأْكُلُونَ	أَكَلْتُمْ	أنتم
كُلْنَ	تَأْكُلْنَ	أَكَلْتُنَّ	أنتنّ
	يَأْكُلُ	أَكَلَ	هو
	تَأْكُلُ	أَكَلَتْ	هي
	يَأْكُلَانِ	أَكَلَا	هما *(masc.)*
	تَأْكُلَانِ	أَكَلَتَا	هما *(fem.)*
	يَأْكُلُونَ	أَكَلُوا	هم
	يَأْكُلْنَ	أَكَلْنَ	هنّ

Other Forms: All other forms are conjugated the same as sound verbs.

تصريف الأفعال المعتلة

Weak Verbs (with a weak letter as first radical) Conjugation

Form I: This type is conjugated exactly like sound verbs. However, the weak letter is dropped in the imperfect tense المضارع and in the imperative الأمر, while it is kept in the perfect tense الماضي.

الأمر	المضارع	الماضي	الضمير
	أَصِلُ	وَصَلْتُ	أنا
	نَصِلُ	وَصَلْنَا	نحن
صِلْ	تَصِلُ	وَصَلْتَ	أنتَ
صِلِي	تَصِلِينَ	وَصَلْتِ	أنتِ
صِلَا	تَصِلَانِ	وَصَلْتُمَا	أنتما
صِلُوا	تَصِلُونَ	وَصَلْتُمْ	أنتم
صِلْنَ	تَصِلْنَ	وَصَلْتُنَّ	أنتنّ
	يَصِلُ	وَصَلَ	هو
	تَصِلُ	وَصَلَتْ	هي
	يَصِلَانِ	وَصَلَا	هما (masc.)
	تَصِلَانِ	وَصَلَتَا	هما (fem.)
	يَصِلُونَ	وَصَلُوا	هم
	يَصِلْنَ	وَصَلْنَ	هنّ

وَصَلَ / يَصِلُ (to arrive)

Other Forms: The other nine forms are conjugated like sound verbs.

الأجوف - المعتل الوسط
Hollow Verbs Conjugation

Form I: There are three patterns of this type:

$$(نَامَ / يَنَامُ) - (قَالَ / يَقُولُ) - (سَارَ / يَسِيرُ)$$

The weak letter (the middle radical) in the three patterns is dropped when followed by (ْ).

The following table shows form I conjugation:

الأمر	المضارع	الماضى	الضمير
قَالَ / يَقُولُ (to say)			
	أَقُولُ	قُلْتُ	أنا
	نَقُولُ	قُلْنَا	نحن
قُلْ	تَقُولُ	قُلْتَ	أنتَ
قُولِي	تَقُولِينَ	قُلْتِ	أنتِ
قُولَا	تَقُولَانِ	قُلْتُمَا	أنتما
قُولُوا	تَقُولُونَ	قُلْتُمْ	أنتم
قُلْنَ	تَقُلْنَ	قُلْتُنَّ	أنتنّ
	يَقُولُ	قَالَ	هو
	تَقُولُ	قَالَتْ	هي
	يَقُولَانِ	قَالَا	هما (masc.)
	تَقُولَانِ	قَالَتَا	هما (fem.)
	يَقُولُونَ	قَالُوا	هم
	يَقُلْنَ	قُلْنَ	هنّ

Other Forms:

1. In forms (**II, III, V, VI and IX**), hollow verbs are conjugated like **sound verbs**.

2. In forms (**IV, VII, VIII and X**), they are conjugated like **hollow verbs - form I** illustrated above, in that the weak letter (the middle radical) is dropped when followed by (ـْ). See the *sukun* rule on page 33.

النّاقص – المعتل الآخر

Conjugation of the Third Type

Form I: There are three patterns:

$$(دَعَا / يَدْعُو) - (مَشَى / يَمْشِي) - (رَضِيَ / يَرْضَى)$$

1. The patterns (دَعَا / يَدْعُو) and (مَشَى / يَمْشِي):

Apply the *sukun* rule and drop the weak letter when it comes before a *sukun* and before long vowels.

The following table shows the conjugation of these types with different pronouns:

الأمر	المضارع	الماضي	الضمير
مَشَى / يَمْشِي (to walk)			
	أَمْشِي	مَشَيْتُ	أنا
	نَمْشِي	مَشَيْنَا	نحن
اِمْشِ	تَمْشِي	مَشَيْتَ	أنتَ
اِمْشِي	تَمْشِينَ	مَشَيْتِ	أنتِ
اِمْشِيَا	تَمْشِيَان	مَشَيْتُمَا	أنتما
اِمْشُوا	تَمْشُونَ	مَشَيْتُمْ	أنتم
اِمْشِينَ	تَمْشِينَ	مَشَيْتُنَّ	أنتنّ
	يَمْشِي	مَشَى	هو
	تَمْشِي	مَشَتْ	هي
	يَمْشِيَان	مَشَيَا	هما (masc.)
	تَمْشِيَان	مَشَتَا	هما (fem.)
	يَمْشُونَ	مَشَوْا	هم
	يَمْشِينَ	مَشَيْنَ	هنّ

2. The pattern (رَضِيَ / يَرْضَى):

Apply the *sukun* rule and drop the weak letter when it comes before a *sukun* and before long vowels.

The following table shows the conjugation of this type with different pronouns:

الأمر	المضارع	الماضي	الضمائر
	رَضِيَ / يَرْضَى (to be content, satisfied)		
	أَرْضَى	رَضِيتُ	أنا
	نَرْضَى	رَضِينَا	نحن
إِرْضَ	تَرْضَى	رَضِيتَ	أنتَ
إِرْضِي	تَرْضَيْنَ	رَضِيتِ	أنتِ
إرْضَيَا	تَرْضَيَانِ	رَضِيتُمَا	أنتما
إِرْضَوْا	تَرْضَوْنَ	رَضِيتُمْ	أنتم
إرْضَيْنَ	تَرْضَيْنَ	رَضِيتُنَّ	أنتنّ
	يَرْضَى	رَضِيَ	هو
	تَرْضَى	رَضِيَتْ	هي
	يَرْضَيَانِ	رَضِيَا	هما (masc.)
	تَرْضَيَانِ	رَضِيَتَا	هما (fem.)
	يَرْضَوْنَ	رَضُوا	هم
	يَرْضَيْنَ	رَضِينَ	هنّ

15

كانَ وأخواتها
Kana and Its Sisters

---

1. كان وأخواتها are verbs that introduce nominal sentences to add new meanings (mostly tense).

2. They are:

   a. كان which places the nominal sentence الجملة الاسمية in the past tense. For example:

   أحمد طالب. (Ahmed is a student.)

   كان أحمدُ طالباً. (Ahmed was a student.)

   b. أصبح (to become). For example:

   أصبح أحمدُ طالباً. (Ahmed has become a student.)

   c. صار (to become). For example:

   صار أحمدُ طالباً. (Ahmed has become a student.)

   d. ظلّ (to continue to be, to keep on). For example:

   ظلّ أحمدُ طالباً. (Ahmed continues to be a student.)

   e. مازال (to continue to be, to keep on). For example:

   مازال أحمدُ طالباً. (Ahmed is still a student.)

   f. ليس (negation: is not). For example:

   ليس أحمدُ طالباً. (Ahmed is not a student.)

g. مادام (as long as). For example:

سأدرس ما دمت حيا. (I will study as long as I am alive.)

h. أضحى - أمسى - بات (to become), but they are not frequently used in Modern Standard Arabic.

3. After كان وأخواتها the subject المبتدأ is in the nominative case مرفوع and it is called الخبر. The predicate اسم كان (أصبح - ظلّ ... إلخ) is in the accusative منصوب and it is called خبر كان (أصبح - صار ... إلخ).

4. As a predicate, خبر كان may be a verbal sentence. In this case, if كان is in the past tense the verb of the predicate must be in the present tense, or the particle قد should be used. Examples:

كان الطالبُ يدرسُ العربيةَ. (The student was studying Arabic.)
كان الطالبُ قد درسَ العربيةَ. (The student had studied Arabic.)

5. كان وأخواتها are called incomplete verbs أفعال ناقصة because they take a predicate and not a direct object. They are also called أفعال ناسخة because they change the case ending of the predicate علامة إعراب الخبر to the accusative منصوب.

6. كان وأخواتها can start a sentence except مادام which must be preceded by a sentence.

7. As verbs, كان وأخواتها are conjugated with different pronouns. Most of them have different tenses as shown in the following table:

الأمر	المستقبل	المضارع	الماضي
كن	سيكون	يكون	كان
أصبح	سيصبح	يصبح	أصبح
صر	سيصير	يصير	صار
ظلّ	سيظلّ	يظلّ	ظلّ
			ليس
			مادام
		لا يزال	ما زال

16

إنَّ وأخواتها
Inna and Its Sisters

1. إنَّ وأخواتها are particles حروف ناسخة that introduce nominal sentences to add different meanings.

2. Their meanings are:

a. إنَّ When it appears at the beginning of a speech, it adds emphasis and/or style to the meaning. It is usually untranslatable. For example:

إنَّ الكتابَ مفيدٌ. ('Indeed' the book is useful.)

b. إنَّ – أنَّ mean 'that.' The difference between them is that: إنَّ is used after the verb قال / يقول, and أنَّ is used elsewhere. Examples:

قال إنَّ الكتابَ مفيد. (He said that the book is useful.)

يبدو أنَّ الكتابَ مفيد. (It seems that the book is useful.)

c. كأنَّ means 'as if, as though.' For example:

الجو حار كأنّنا في الصيف. (It is hot as if we are in summer.)

d. لكنَّ means 'but.' For example:

أنا مدرسةٌ لكنَّ أحمدَ طبيبٌ. (I am a teacher but Ahmed is a doctor.)

e. لعلَّ means 'perhaps.' For example:

لعلَّ صديقي يصل في الميعاد. (Perhaps my friend would arrive on time.)

f. ‏ليت‎ means 'I wish.' For example:

‏ليت صديقي يصل في الميعاد.‎ (I wish that my friend arrives on time.)

3. ‏إنَّ وأخواتها‎ are called ‏حروف ناسخة‎ because they change the case ending of the subject ‏المبتدأ‎ ‏علامة إعراب‎ to be in the accusative ‏منصوب‎.

4. After ‏إنَّ وأخواتها‎, the subject ‏المبتدأ‎ is in the accusative case ‏منصوب‎, and it is called ‏اسم إنَّ‎. The predicate ‏الخبر‎ is in the nominative case ‏مرفوع‎, and it is called ‏خبر إنَّ‎. For example:

‏الكتابُ مفيدٌ. — إنَّ الكتابَ مفيدٌ.‎

5. ‏إنَّ وأخواتها‎ can begin a sentence except ‏لكنَّ - أنَّ‎ which must be preceded by a sentence.

17

كاد وأخواتها

Kada and Its Sisters

أفعال المقاربة   (كاد - أوشك - قرب)
أفعال الرجاء   (عسى - حرى - اخلولق)
أفعال الشروع   (أخذ - جعل - بدأ - أنشأ - شرع - طفق - هبّ)

1. كاد وأخواتها are verbs which introduce nominal sentences in order to add different meanings. (The underlined verbs are the most commonly used in Modern Standard Arabic.)

2. كاد and أوشك mean that something (the predicate) is about to happen. For example:

كاد جون يعرف اللغة العربية.

(John is about to know the Arabic language.)

On the other hand, عسى means that it is wished that something given by the predicate happens. For example:

عسى المتعلمون أن يتقنوا اللغة العربية.

(Let us hope that learners master Arabic.)

3. أخذ and جعل mean that the subject continues to do something. For example: أخذ الرجلُ يعمل. (The man kept working.)

4. بدأ means that the subject starts to do something. For example: بدأ الرجلُ يعمل. (The man starts working.)

5. When adding كاد وأخواتها to a nominal sentence, the subject المبتدأ remains nominative and is called اسم كاد, while the predicate الخبر is called خبر كاد.

6. The predicate الخبر must be a verbal sentence with a verb in the imperfect tense مضارع.

7. In the case of using أوشك and عسى, the imperfect tense verb (the predicate الخبر) must be preceded by the particle أنْ. For example:

أوشك جون أن يتعلم اللغة العربية.

8. Only كاد and أوشك may be used in the imperfect tense (يكاد and يوشك).

9. كاد وأخواتها are verbs and must agree with their subjects according to the rules of verb conjugation. Examples:

كاد الطالب ينتهي من الدراسة.
كادت الطالبة تنتهي من الدراسة.
الطلاب كادوا ينتهون من الدراسة.

18

بناء الفعل للمجهول
Passive Voice

In verbal sentences, while the subject الفاعل of an active verb performs the act denoted by the verb, the subject نائب الفاعل of a passive verb is acted upon by an unnamed agent.

In order to change the verbal sentence from active voice المبني للمعلوم to passive voice المبني للمجهول, we must follow the following steps:

1. The form of the verb is changed as follows:

   a. الفعل الماضي:

   - Change the first vowel to (ُ) if short, and (و) if long.

   - The vowel before the last is changed to (ِ) or (ي).

   $$\text{فَتَحَ} \rightarrow \text{فُتِح} \qquad \text{قَابَل} \rightarrow \text{قُوبِل}$$
   $$\text{صَام} \rightarrow \text{صِيمَ} \qquad \text{اسْتَفَاد} \rightarrow \text{اسْتُفِيدَ}$$

   b. الفعل المضارع:

   - Change the first vowel to (ُ).

   - The vowel before the last is changed to (َ) or (ا).

   $$\text{يَفْتَحُ} \rightarrow \text{يُفْتَحُ} \qquad \text{يَجِدُ} \rightarrow \text{يُوجَدُ}$$
   $$\text{يَسْتَخْرِجُ} \rightarrow \text{يُسْتَخْرَجُ} \qquad \text{يَسْتَفِيد} \rightarrow \text{يُسْتَفَادُ}$$

2. الفاعل is removed and replaced by المفعول به, which is then called نائب الفاعل and becomes مرفوع.

   $$\text{كتبَ الطالبُ الدرسَ.} \rightarrow \text{كُتِبَ الدرسُ.}$$

3. The conjugation of passive verbs is exactly like that of active verbs.

19

جزم ونصب الفعل المضارع
Jussive and Subjunctive

الفعل المضارع (the imperfect tense verb) is مرفوع (indicative) unless it is introduced by one of the particles which change its mood to الجزم (jussive) or النصب (subjunctive).

الفعل المضارع المرفوع (indicative) is marked as follows:

1. (ْ) with the pronouns: أنا – نحن – أنتَ – هو – هي

    أنا أكتبُ – نحن نكتبُ – أنت تكتبُ – هو يكتبُ – هي تكتبُ

2. (ن) with the pronouns: أنتِ – أنتما – أنتم – هما – هم

    أنت تكتبين – أنتما تكتبان – أنتم تكتبون – هما يكتبان – هما تكتبان – هم يكتبون

3. الفعل المضارع is مبنيّ (indeclinable) with the pronouns أنتنّ – هنّ

    أنتن تكتبن – هن يكتبن

جزم الفعل المضارع
Jussive of the Imperfect Tense

First: The imperfect tense is put in the jussive form when preceded by one of the following particles:

1. لم النافية (of negation). لم يكتبْ (He did not write.)
2. لا الناهية (of prohibition). لا تكتبْ (Do not write.)
3. لـ الأمر (of command). لتكتبْ (Write.)
4. لمّا النافية (of negation). اليوم الامتحان ولمّا تدرسوا (Today is the exam and you haven't studied.)

5. Some conditional particles (see the section on 'conditional sentences' for an explanation of these.)

Second: الفعل المجزوم is marked as follows:

1. Sound verbs have a *sukun* over the last radical when they are singular. For example:

يَكتبُ changes to لم يكتبْ

2. Weak letters are dropped from singular defective verbs. For example:

يقُولُ changes to لم يقُلْ
يَمْشِي changes to لم يَمْشِ

3. The (ن) as a marker of dual, plural masculine, and second person singular feminine is dropped. For example:

يكتبان changes to لم يكتبا
تكتبان changes to لم تكتبا
يكتبون changes to لم يكتبوا
تكتبون changes to لم تكتبوا
تكتبين changes to لم تكتبي

نصب الفعل المضارع
The Subjunctive of the Imperfect

First: An imperfect verb is in the subjunctive mood when preceded by one of the following particles:

1. أنْ. Examples: أريد أنْ أكتبَ. (I want to write.)
يجب أنْ أذاكرَ. (It is necessary that I study.)

2. لَنْ. Example: لن أنامَ. (I will not sleep.)

3. كَيْ - لِـ - حَتَّى. For example:

ذاكر (كي - حتى - ل) تنجَحَ. (Study in order to succeed.)

4. فَـ. For example: ذاكر فتنجحَ. (Study, and so you succeed.)

Second: الفعل المنصوب is marked as follows:

1. Singular verbs have fatha (◌َ) over the last radical. Examples:

يكتبُ	changes to	لن يكتبَ
يقولُ	changes to	لن يقولَ

2. The (ن) as a marker of dual, plural masculine and second person singular feminine is dropped. Examples:

يكتبان	changes to	لن يكتبا
تكتبان	changes to	لن تكتبا
يكتبون	changes to	لن يكتبوا
تكتبون	changes to	لن تكتبوا
تكتبين	changes to	لن تكتبي

20

النفي
Negation

أولاً: نفي الجملة الفعلية
First: Negation of Verbal Sentences

1. Perfect Tense (الماضي):

Negation of the perfect tense is expressed in one of two ways:

1. ما + الماضي (perfect + ما)
2. لم + المضارع المجزوم (jussive + لم)

For example:

ما كتبَ الطالب . or لم يكتبْ الطالب . :is negated as كتبَ الطالب .

2. Imperfect Tense (المضارع):

The imperfect tense is negated by the negative particle (لا). For example:

لا يكتبُ الطالب . :is negated as يكتبُ الطالب .

3. Future Tense (المستقبل):

Negation of the future tense is expressed by adding the negative particle (لن) and dropping the future prefix. For example:

لن يكتبَ الطالب . :are negated as سيكتب الطالب . and سوف يكتبُ الطالب .

The verb after لن is subjunctive منصوب.

ثانياً: نفي الجملة الإسمية

Second: Negation of Nominal Sentences

1. Nominal sentence with a noun, *idaafa* construction, adverbial phrase, or prepositional phrase as predicate:

This is expressed by using the verb (ليس) which is one of the sisters of (كان).

This verb follows the usual rules of verb conjugation in that:

a. If the verb precedes the subject, only gender agreement is required. For example:

الطلاب في الفصل. is negated as: ليس الطلاب في الفصل.

b. If the verb follows the subject, gender and number agreement are required. For example:

الطلاب في الفصل. can be negated as: الطلاب ليسوا في الفصل.

2. Nominal sentence with verbal sentence as predicate:

This is expressed by negating the verb following the usual rules of negating verbs. It is preferable for stylistic reasons to change the nominal sentence to a verbal one. Examples:

الطالب كتب   is negated as: لم يكتبْ الطالبُ. or الطالب لم يكتب.

الطالب يكتب   is negated as: لا يكتبُ الطالبُ. or الطالب لا يكتب.

الطالب سيكتب   is negated as: لن يكتبَ الطالبُ. or الطالب لن يكتب.

ثالثاً: نفي الأسماء والصفات

Third: Negation of Nouns and Adjectives

1. The use of (لا) for absolute negation:

لا (النافية للجنس) is used to negate a noun (not a sentence like ليس).

It is followed by an indefinite noun in the accusative case and without nunation. Examples:

لا شكَّ. (There is no doubt.)

لا أحدَ في الفصل. (There is no one in the class.)

2. The use of (غير):

a. غير is a noun used to express two meanings:

b. One meaning is 'other than.' For example:

درست العربية وغيرها. (I studied Arabic and other languages.)

c. It is also used to negate nouns and adjectives and may be translated 'non-, un-, etc.' It forms with the noun following it an *idaafa*, and the noun is then genitive مجرور. Examples:

طلاب غير عربٍ (non-Arab students)

مطرب غير معروفٍ (unknown singer)

3. The use of (عدم):

It is used to negate nouns; specifically, verbal nouns المصادر. It may be translated as (no, non-, lack of, etc.) Like غير, and it forms an *idaafa* with the noun following it, and the noun is then genitive مجرور. Examples:

الانحياز (taking the side of)	ة	عدم الانحيازِ (non-alignment)
الوجود (existence)	ة	عدم الوجودِ (non-existence)
النوم (sleeping)	ة	عدم النومِ (lack of sleep)

4. Negated Question:

The particle (أ) is used. Examples:

ألم تدرس العربية؟

أليس هذا كتابك؟

21

الأسماء الموصولة

Relative Pronouns

	Masculine	Feminine
Singular	الَّذي	الَّتي
Dual nom. accusative / genetive	اللَّذان اللَّذَيْنِ	الْلَتَانِ الْلَتَيْنِ
Plural	الَّذينَ	اللَّوَاتي - الْلَاتي - الْلَائي
Non human (indefinite)		مَا
Human (indefinite)		مَنْ

1   The relative pronoun الاسم الموصول introduces a sentence called the relative clause جملة الصلة, and refers to an antecedent موصول which must be definite. For example:

الكتاب الّذي قرأته مفيد جدا.

2.   The function of the relative pronoun is to join the relative clause with the antecedent.

3.   The relative pronoun must agree with the antecedent in gender, number, and case. Note that case is distinguished only in the dual. Examples:

هذان هما الكتابان اللذان قرأتهما.
قرأت القصتين اللتين ألفهما هذا الكاتب.

4. The relative clause is an adjectival clause modifying the antecedent.

5. There must be a pronoun, in the relative clause referring to the antecedent, called a presumptive pronoun ضمير العائد. For example:

الكتاب الذي قرأتهِ مفيد .

6. ضمير العائد may be one of the following types:

هذا هو الكاتب الّذي كتب الكتاب : مستتر Latent

هذا هو الكتاب الّذي قرأتهِ . Object of a verb.

هذا هو الكتاب الذي بحثت عنهِ . Object of a preposition.

هذا هو الكتاب الذي كاتبهِ مشهور . Suffixed to a noun.

7. ضمير العائد must agree in number and gender with the antecedent.
Examples:

الكتابَ الذي قرأتهِ مفيد .

القصة التي قرأتها مفيدة .

الكتابان اللذان قرأتهما مفيدان .

8. When the verb takes a preposition, ضمير العائد should be attached to
the preposition. For example:

وجدت الكتابَ الذي كنت أبحث عنهِ .

9. ما and من are relative pronouns which include their antecedents within
themselves. Therefore, they never have a specified antecedent. Examples:

قابلت من ألّف الكتاب . (I met with he who wrote the book.)

رأيت ما فعلوه أمس . (I saw what they did yesterday.)

10. When the object of the verb after ما or من refers to either of them, it
is optional to attach a presumptive pronoun ضمير العائد to the verb. For
example:

رأيت ما فعلوه أمس . ــ رأيت ما فعلوا أمس .

22

الأسماء الخمسة
The Five Nouns

1. الأسماء الخمسة are nouns which have a special nature when they are followed by other nouns in إضافة. They are:

- أبو - (The father of)
- أخو - (The brother of)
- حمو - (The father-in-law of)
- فو - (The mouth of)
- ذو - (He who is characterized with)

2. The most commonly used of these nouns are: أبو - أخو - ذو.

3. The special thing about these nouns is that they take (و - ا - ي) as endings for different cases. The following table shows their forms in different cases:

الجر	النصب	الرفع
ذي	ذا	ذو
أبي	أبا	أبو
أخي	أخا	أخو
حمي	حما	حمو
في	فا	فو

For example: هذا هو أبو أحمد. — قابلت أبا أحمد. — تكلمت مع أبي أحمد.

4. When the pronominal suffix (ي ‪-‬ my) ياء المتكلم is attached, these nouns do not take different case endings. For example:

هذا هو أبي. — قابلت أبي. — تكلمت مع أبي.

5. When they are not in an *idaafa*, they take تنوين (‪ٍ‬ ‪-‬ ‪ً‬ ‪-‬ ‪ٌ‬) like normal nouns. For example:

إنه أخٌ كريم. — عرفت أخاً كريما. — تحدثت إلى أخٍ كريم.

6. الأسماء الخمسة can be changed to dual and plural like other nouns. The following table shows their forms in different cases:

جمع	مثنى	
ذَوُو	ذَوَا	حالة الرفع
ذَوِي	ذَوَيْ	حالتا النصب والجر

For example:

هذان هما أخوا أحمد. — قابلت أخوي أحمد. — تكلمت مع أخوي أحمد.

7. (ذو) is always used in an *idaafa*, and cannot be attached to pronouns. The feminine form is (ذات), which takes (‪ٍ‬ ‪-‬ ‪ِ‬ ‪-‬ ‪ٌ‬) like normal nouns. It is not considered to be among the five nouns.

8. The dual forms of ذات are: ذواتا for nominative ذواتي for accusative and genitive.

9. The plural of ذات is ذوات. Like all sound feminine plural nouns, it takes (‪ٌ‬) in the nominative case and (‪ٍ‬) in the accusative and genitive cases.

23

الإسم المقصور والإسم المنقوص
Abbreviated and Defective Nouns

أولاً: الاسم المقصور
First: Abbreviated Noun

1. The last radical is pronounced (ا) whether it is written (ا) or (ى), such as:

الفتَى — العصَا

2. The noun takes تنوين when it is indefinite, but it does not change in any case as shown below:

نكرة	معرفة	الحالة الإعرابية
جاء فتًى.	جاء الفتى.	مرفوع
قابلت فتًى.	قابلت الفتى.	منصوب
تكلمت مع فتًى.	تكلمت مع الفتى.	مجرور

ثانياً: الاسم المنقوص
Second: Defective Noun

1. The last radical is (ي) preceded by a *kasra*, such as:

القاضِي — المحامِي — الوادِي

2. The noun takes تنوين when it is indefinite, and has **only** two case endings as shown below:

نكرة	معرفة	الحالة الإعرابية
جاء قاضٍ.	جاء القاضي.	مرفوع - مجرور
سرت في وادٍ.	سرت في الوادي.	
قابلت قاضياً.	قابلت القاضيَ.	منصوب

3. When the defective noun الاسم المنقوص is plural, it does not take تنوين in the accusative.

نكرة	معرفة	الحالة الإعرابية
هذه أغانٍ عربية.	الأغاني العربية جميلة.	مرفوع - مجرور
جلسنا على كراسٍ.	جلسنا على الكراسي.	
سمعنا أغانيَ عربية.	سمعنا الأغانيَ العربية.	منصوب

24

المنوع من الصرف
Diptotes

---

1. In Arabic, singular nouns and broken plurals have a kasra (ِ) for the genitive case, and a *fatha* (َ) for the accusative case, and have nunation تنوين as a marker for indefiniteness.

2. Some nouns have a *fatha* (َ) for both the genitive and the accusative cases, and do not have nunation تنوين. Those nouns are called diptotes المنوع من الصرف.

3. When diptotes have the definite article or when they are the first term of an *idaafa*, these nouns take *kasra* (ِ) for the genitive case like normal nouns, but they do not take nunation تنوين.

4. The table on the following page shows the different types of the diptotes.

5. Besides the nouns shown in the table, the following nouns are diptotes:

    a. All feminine nouns ending in ألف مقصورة. Examples:

ذكرى ــ سلوى ــ عطشى

    b. All nouns ending in اء when (ء) is not a radical of the root: Examples:

أنبياء ــ أصدقاء ــ صحراء

صيغة منتهى الجموع *Plurals*	الصفة *Adjectives*	العلم *Proper nouns*
على وزن (أفاعل): أفاضل - أجانب	على وزن (فعلان) مؤنثه فعلى: عطشان - جوعان - شبعان	مؤنث *(Feminine)*: فاطمة - مكة - سعاد - زينب - بغداد - دمشق
على وزن (أفاعيل): أناشيد - أساطير	على وزن (أفعل): أفضل - أكبر - أحمر - أخضر	علم أعجمي *(Foreign names)*: إبراهيم - جيمس - يعقوب - سيمون
على وزن (فعائل): طبائع - رسائل	من ١: ١٠ على وزن (مفعل - فعال): مثنى - ثلاث - رباع	مركب تركيا مزجيا *(Synthetic compound)*: بورسعيد - نيويورك
على وزن (مفاعل): مدارس - ملاعب	جمع أخرى: أخر	في آخره ألف ونون: مروان - عثمان
على وزن (مفاعيل): مفاتيح - مناديل		على وزن الفعل: أحمد - يزيد
على وزن (فواعل): شوارع - سواعد		على وزن (فعل): عمر - قزح
على وزن (فعاليل): عصافير		

Important Notes:

1. If the *hamza* of the ending ءا **is a part of the root**, the noun is considered regular and it takes *kasra* and *tanween*, such as:

سماء (سمو) ــ بناء (بني) ــ أشياء (شيء)

2. Feminine nouns with *sukun* (ْ) on the second of three radicals may be considered diptotes or regular nouns, such as:

مِصْر ــ هِنْد

25

المصدر
Verbal Nouns

1. The verbal noun is a noun indicating the basic meaning of the verb without tense. For example:

كتابة (writing)

2. Verbal nouns function as other nouns in that they can be subjects, objects, predicates, etc.

3. The meaning of the verbal noun can be expressed through the structure أنْ + الفعل.

4. أن is called حرف مصدري (infinitival particle) which, with the verb, can replace the verbal noun. أنْ + الفعل = المصدر

أنْ يستخدم = استخدام

5. Except form I verbs, the verbal nouns are predictable within each form. They are formed according to specific patterns.

6. When المصدر is used to indicate the meaning of 'doing,' it has to be definite.

Form I

Following are some examples of the verbal nouns of form I verbs

المعنى	المصدر	الفعل
To read	قِرَاءَة	قرأ / يقرأ
To write	كتابة	كتب / يكتب
To study	دراسة	درس / يدرس
To visit	زيارة	زار / يزور
To drive	قيادة	قاد / يقود
To swim	سباحة	سبح / يسبح
To take care of	رعاية	رعى / يرعى
To guard	حراسة	حرس / يحرس
To sit down	جُلُوس	جلس / يجلس
To stand up	وقوف	وقف / يقف
To arrive	وصول	وصل / يصل
To return	رجوع	رجع / يرجع
To enter	دخول	دخل / يدخل
To exit	خروج	خرج / يخرج
To come, to attend	حضور	حضر / يحضر
To ride	ركوب	ركب / يركب
To go down	نزول	نزل / ينزل
To go down, to descend	هبوط	هبط / يهبط
To go up	طلوع	طلع / يطلع
To go up, to ascend	صعود	صعد / يصعد
To fall	وقوع	وقع / يقع
To fall	سقوط	سقط / يسقط
To get up, to rise	نهوض	نهض / ينهض
To pass	مرور	مرّ / يمرّ

المعنى	المصدر	الفعل
To put	وَضْع	وضع / يضع
To pay, to push	دفع	دفع / يدفع
To hit	ضرب	ضرب / يضرب
To prevent	منع	منع / يمنع
To fill	ملئ	ملأ / يملأ
To eat	أكل	أكل / يأكل
To open	فتح	فتح / يفتح
To cook	طبخ	طبخ / يطبخ
To uncover	كشف	كشف / يكشف
To examine	فحص	فحص / يفحص
To lift, to raise	رفع	رفع / يرفع
To take	أخذ	أخذ / يأخذ
To hear	سمع	سمع / يسمع
To cut	قطع	قطع / يقطع
To break	كسر	كسر / يكسر
To make a reservation	حجز	حجز / يحجز
To draw	رسم	رسم / يرسم
To collect	جمع	جمع / يجمع
To explain	شرح	شرح / يشرح
To transmit	نقل	نقل / ينقل
To publish	نشر	نشر / ينشر
To weigh	وزن	وزن / يزن
To run	جري	جرى / يجري
To walk	مشي	مشى / يمشي

المعنى	المصدر	الفعل
To say	قول	قال / يقول
To get up	صحو	صحا / يصحو
To sleep	نوم	نام / ينام
To fast	صوم	صام / يصوم
To walk	سير	سار / يسير
To count	عدّ	عدّ / يعدّ
To stretch, to extend	مدّ	مدّ / يمدّ
To pull	شدّ	شدّ / يشدّ
To give back, to reply	ردّ	ردّ / يردّ
To prevent, to block	سدّ	سدّ / يسدّ
To smell	شمّ	شمّ / يشمّ
To drink	شُرب	شرب / يشرب
To thank	شكر	شكر / يشكر
To go	ذهاب	ذهب / يذهب
To permit, to allow	سماح	سمح / يسمح
To build	بناء	بنى / يبني
To judge	قضاء	قضى / يقضي
To meet	لقاء	لقي / يلقى
To beg, to hope	رجاء	رجا / يرجو
To ask	سُؤَال	سأل / يسأل
To work, to do	عَمَل	عمل / يعمل
To reside	سكن	سكن / يسكن
To see	رُؤْيَة	رأى / يرى
To return	عودة	عاد / يعود

المعنى	المصدر	الفعل
To serve	خدمة	خدم / يخدم

Form II

1. It has the pattern تَفْعِيل. For example:

درّس / يدرّس ➡ تدريس (To teach).

2. If the third radical of the verb is a weak letter, the pattern is then تَفْعِلَة
For example:

سمّى / يسمّي ➡ تسمية (To name).

Form III

1. It has the pattern مُفَاعَلَة. For example:

ساعد / يساعد ➡ مساعدة (To help).

2. If the third radical of the verb is a weak letter, it is changed to (١). For
example:

نادى / ينادي ➡ مناداة (To call out).

Form IV

1. It has the pattern إِفْعَال. For example:

أكمل / يكمل ➡ إكمال (To complete).

2. If the first radical of the verb is a weak letter, it is changed to (ـي). For
example:

أوقف / يوقف ➡ إيقاف (To stop).

3. If the second radical of the verb is a weak letter, the vowel is dropped and ـة is added. For example:

(To help) أعان / يعين ➜ إعانة

4. If the third radical of the verb is a weak letter, it is changed to (ء). For example:

(To give) أعطى / يعطي ➜ إعطاء

Form V

1. It has the pattern تَفَعُّل. For example:

(To expect) توقّع / يتوقّع ➜ توقّع

2. If the third radical of the verb is a weak letter, the rules of الاسم المنقوص are applied. For example:

(To wish) تمنّى / يتمنّى ➜ تمنٍ - التمني

Form VI

1. It has the pattern تَفَاعُل. For example:

(To cooperate) تعاون / يتعاون ➜ تعاون

2. If the third radical of the verb is a weak letter, the rules of الاسم المنقوص are applied. For example:

(To come to terms) تراضى / يتراضى ➜ تراضٍ - التراضي

Form VII

1. It has the pattern اِنْفِعَال. For example:

(To leave, to go away) انصرف / ينصرف ➜ انصراف

2. If the third radical of the verb is a weak letter, it is changed to (ء). For example:

(To pass). انقضى / ينقضي � انقضاء

Form VIII

1. It has the pattern اِفْتِعَال. For example:

(To confess). اعترف / يعترف ➡ اعتراف

2. If the third radical of the verb is a weak letter, it is changed to (ء). For example:

(To commit an aggression). اعتدى / يعتدي ➡ اعتداء

Form IX

1. It has the pattern اِفْعِلَال. For example:

(To turn red). احمرّ / يحمرّ ➡ احمرار

Form X

1. It has the pattern اِسْتِفْعَال. For example:

(To receive). استقبل / يستقبل ➡ استقبال

2. If the middle radical of the verb is a weak letter, (ة) is added. For example:

(To resign). استقال / يستقيل ➡ استقالة

3. If the last radical is a weak letter, it is changed to (ء). For example:

(To call). استدعى / يستدعي ➡ استدعاء

26

اسم الفاعل

Active Participles

1. اسم الفاعل is the noun indicating the doer of the action denoted by the verb. For example:

كاتب = الشخص الذي يكتب (writer = the person who writes)

2. It is derived from verbs as follows:

Form I Verbs

1. The pattern is فَاعِل regardless of the stem vowel of the underlying verb. For example:

كاتب ← كتب / يكتب

لاعب ← لعب / يلعب

2. If the middle radical is (ا) it turns into (ء). For example:

نائم ← نام / ينام

قائم ← قام / يقوم

Other Verb Forms

All active participles of verbs other than form I are formed from the pattern of the imperfect tense, but they begin with (مُ) instead of the prefix, and have a *kasra* (ِ) before the last radical, except form IX which has a *fatha* (َ). For example:

Form II	درّس / يدرّس	مُدرّس	(To teach)
Form III	لاحظ / يلاحظ	مُلاحِظ	(To notice)
Form IV	أرسل / يرسل	مُرسِل	(To send)
Form V	تأكّد / يتأكّد	مُتأكِّد	(To be sure)
Form VI	تعاون / يتعاون	مُتعاوِن	(To be cooperative)
Form VII	انفعل / ينفعل	مُنفعِل	(To be excited)
Form VIII	اقترب / يقترب	مُقترِب	(To be near)
Form IX	احمرّ / يحمرّ	مُحمرّ	(To become red)
Form X	استقبل / يستقبل	مُستقبِل	(To receive)

Note: If the third radical is a vowel, the rules of الاسم المنقوص are applied.
Examples:

مضى / يمضي ➜ ماضٍ - الماضي

اشترى / يشتري ➜ مشترٍ - المشتري

27

اسم المفعول
Passive Participles

1. The basic meaning of اسم المفعول is a noun undergoing the action denoted by the verb.

2. It is derived as follows:

Form I Verbs

1. The pattern is مَفْعُول. For example:

كتب / يكتب   ➡   مكتوب

لعب / يلعب   ➡   ملعوب

2. Hollow verbs:

باع / يبيع   ➡   مبيع

لام / يلوم   ➡   ملوم

3. Defective verbs:

بنى / يبني   ➡   مبنيّ

دعا / يدعو   ➡   مدعوّ

Other Verb Forms:

All passive participles of verbs other than form I are made from the pattern of the imperfect tense, but they begin with (مُ) instead of the first letter, and have a *fatha* (ﹷ) before the last radical. For example:

Form II	مُدرّس	درّس / يدرّس
Form III	مُلاحَظ	لاحظ / يلاحظ
Form IV	مُرسَل	أرسل / يرسل
Form V	مُتقبّل	تقبّل / يتقبّل
Form VI	مُتبادَل	تبادل / يتبادل
Form VII	rare	
Form VIII	مُتّفَق	اتّفق / يتّفق
Form IX	rare	
Form X	مُستقبَل	استقبل / يستقبل

Note: If the third radical is a weak letter, the rules of الاسم المقصور are applied: Examples:

سمّى / يسمّي ➜ مسمّى

أعطى / يعطي ➜ معطى

اسم المكانْ
Nouns of Place

1. اسم المكان is a noun derived from a verb to indicate the place where the action denoted by the verb is taking place.

2. In most cases, this is made from form I verbs according to the pattern مَفعَل. For example:

مكتب — ملعب — مدرسة

3. When a form I verb in the imperfect tense has the vowel (ِ) and the middle radical and the third radical are consonants, اسم المكان is formed according to the pattern مَفعِل. For example:

مجلس — موعد — مضرب

4. With other verb forms, اسم المكان is formed according to the pattern of اسم المفعول. For example:

مستشفى — مستودع

الحـال

Accusative of State

1. الحَال is an accusative اسم منصوب that modifies and describes the condition of a noun, or the circumstances surrounding it **at the time of the action** denoted by the verb.

2. The difference between الحَال and الصفة is that الحَال is **changeable from time to time.** Examples:

حضر الطالبُ السعيدُ. (صفة) (The happy student came.)

حضر الطالبُ سعيداً. (حال) (The student came happily.)

3. There are three types of الحَال:

a. An adjective: In this case, it must be accusative منصوب, and indefinite. For example:

جاء الطالب سعيداً. (The student came happily.)

b. A sentence:

1. A nominal sentence: It must be preceded by (و). For example:

جاء إلى مصر وهو صغير. (He came to Egypt while he was young.)

2. A verbal sentence:

■ **Perfect:** It must be preceded by (و)

- Affirmative preceded by (قد). For example:

رجع إلى بلده وقد أكمل دراسته الجامعية.

(He returned to his country having completed his university studies.)

- Negated by (ما) or (لم). For example:

رجع إلى بلاده ولم يكملْ دراسته الجامعية.

(He returned to his country without completing his
university studies.)

■ **Imperfect:** without using (و)

- Affirmative. For example:

رجع إلى بلده يحمل رسالة هامة.

(He returned to his country carrying an important letter.)

- Negated by (لا). For example:

رجع إلى بلده لا يحمل أية رسائل.

(He returned to his country not carrying any letters.)

c. **A prepositional or an adverbial phrase.** For example:

وصل وزير الخارجية على رأس الوفد.

(The minister of foreign affairs arrived heading the delegation.)

30

المفعول المطلق
Accusative of Cognate

---

1. المفعول المطلق is a verbal noun which follows its corresponding verb to serve as an adverbial modifier of the verb. It answers the question: How, or how many times, is the action denoted by the verb performed?

2. It is always in the accusative case منصوب.

3. It has to be indefinite unless it is an *idaafa*, in which case it must be definite.

4. The function of المفعول المطلق is to express:
   a. emphasis تأكيد الفعل. For example:

   فهمت الدرس فهماً.

   b. the kind or manner نوع الفعل. For example:

   فهمت الدرس أحسنَ الفهمِ.

   c. enumeration عدد مرات حدوث الفعل. For example:

   قرأت الدرس ثلاثَ مراتٍ.

5. It may occur alone as in 4.a., or may be modified by:
   a. an adjective. For example:

   فهمت الدرس فهماً جيداً.

b. another noun in an *idaafa*. Examples:

فهمت الدرس كلَّ الفهمِ.

فهمت الدرس بعضَ الفهمِ.

فهمت الدرس أحسنَ الفهمِ.

The modifier may occur by itself without المفعول المطلق, in which case it is called نائب المفعول المطلق. Examples:

فهمت الدرس فهماً جيداً. — فهمت الدرس جيداً.

31

المفعول لأجله
Accusative of Cause or Purpose

1. المفعول لأجله is the verbal noun used to express the cause or purpose for the action denoted by the verb.

2. The meaning of المفعول لأجله is 'because of,' 'out of,' or 'in order to.' For example:

يكتب الإنسان الرسائل إلى أصدقائه حباً فيهم .

(People write letters to their friends out of love.)

3. When verbal nouns function as مفعول لأجله, they are put in the accusative case منصوب.

4. If the verbal noun has an object, the object must be placed after a preposition.

5. If there is a preposition usually associated with the object of the verb, that preposition is used; otherwise (لـ) is used. Examples:

ذهب للتسوق بحثا عن شئ معين .

(He went shopping in search of a specific thing.)

سمي طه حسين عميدا للأدب العربي تكريما لَه .

(Taha Husayn was named "the Dean of Arabic Literature" in order to honor him.)

6. When a verb comes after (لِ or كى), it also indicates the cause or purpose for the action denoted by the first verb. However, this construction is not considered مفعول لأجله.

7. These particles are called (لـ and كي (كي التعليل ولام التعليل of causation).

8. Imperfect verbs after these particles are subjunctive. For example:

سمي طه حسين عميد الأدب العربي ليكرم.

Important note:

المفعول لأجله is not formed from all verbs.

32

المفعول فيه (ظرفُ الزمانُ - ظرفُ المكانُ)

Adverbials of Time and Place

1. Adverbials of time and place ظروف الزمان والمكان are accusative nouns أسماء منصوبة, expressing the place or time of performing the action conveyed by the verb in a sentence.

2. Adverbials of time ظروف الزمان are nouns expressing the time of the action. They answer the question "When?" For example:

الآن - ساعة - يوم - قبل - طوال - اليوم - أحيانا - غدا - أسبوع - شهر - سنة
- صباح - مساء - ظهر - ليل - لحظة - قبل - بعد - خلال - أثناء - مدة - فترة

3. Adverbials of place ظروف المكان are nouns expressing the place in which the action is performed. They answer the question "Where?" For example:

وسط - داخل - بين - عند - خلف - أمام - يمين - يسار - شمال - جنوب - شرق
- غرب - تحت - فوق تجاه - حول - قرب

4. Adverbials of place and time ظروف المكان والزمان are of two types:
   a. The first type can be used as adverbs or as normal nouns that function like any other noun in a sentence.

Examples as adverbs: سأزورك يومَ الجمعة.
Examples as normal nouns: يومُ الجمعة إجازة.

b. The second type can be used as adverbs **only**. For example:

حين - بعد - أثناء - خلال - طوال - وراء - خلف - فوق - تحت - بين - عند
- لدى - تجاه - نحو - حول

5. Some adverbs are indeclinable, so their endings never change. For example:

حيثُ - أمسِ - الآنَ - هنَا - هناكَ

*Idaafa*s with كل as the first term are very common as adverbials of time. For example:

كلَّ صباحٍ - كلَّ مساءٍ - كلَّ سنةٍ

33

التمييز
Accusative of Specification

1. التمييز is an indefinite and accusative noun (اسم نكرة منصوب) which clarifies the ambiguity in a sentence.

امتلأ الكوب . (بماذا؟) The glass is full. (of what?)

محمد أفضل من علي . (من أي ناحية؟) Muhammad is better than Ali. (in terms of what?)

2. If we want to clarify the ambiguity of the previous two sentences, the use of التمييز is obligatory.

امتلأ الكوب شاياً . (The glass is full of tea.)

محمد أفضل من أحمد علماً . (Muhammad is better than Ahmad in knowledge.)

3. التمييز must also be used after numerals and is called تمييز العدد as follows:

a. Numbers 3 – 10: تمييز العدد is plural, indefinite, and genitive جمع نكرة مجرور . For example:

ثلاث نساءٍ — ثلاثة رجالٍ .

b. Numbers 11– 99: تمييز العدد is singular, indefinite, and accusative مفرد نكرة منصوب . For example:

خمس عشرة طالبةً — خمسة عشر طالباً

c. Hundreds and thousands: تمييز العدد is singular, indefinite, and genitive مفرد نكرة مجرور . Examples:

مائة طالبٍ — مائة طالبةٍ — ألف طالبٍ — ألف طالبةٍ

تمييز العدد
Nouns Specifying Numerals

Numbers 1–2:

The singular or the dual noun alone is used, or followed by the numeral for emphasis.

Singular noun:

طالبة – طالبة واحدة   طالب – طالب واحد

Dual:

(مرفوع)	طالبان اثنان	طالبان
(مرفوع)	طالبتان اثنتان	طالبتان
(منصوب-مجرور)	طالبين اثنين	طالبين
(منصوب-مجرور)	طالبتين اثنتين	طالبتين

Numbers 3–10:

An *idaafa* construction is used in which the first term is a numeral that is variable (as to case), and the counted noun التمييز is the second term and is genitive. The numeral disagrees with the noun in gender.

ثلاثة طلاب	ثلاث طالبات
أربعة طلاب	أربع طالبات
خمسة طلاب	خمس طالبات
سبعة طلاب	سبع طالبات
ثمانية طلاب	ثماني طالبات
تسعة طلاب	تسع طالبات
عشرة طلاب	عشر طالبات

Numbers 11–12:

The counted noun and the numerals agree in gender. The counted noun التمييز

and the two elements of the numerals are always accusative منصوب except
the first element in twelve (the unit number), which is variable (as to case).

	أحد عشر طالبا	إحدى عشرة طالبة
(مرفوع)	اثنا عشر طالبا	اثنتا عشرة طالبة
(منصوب - مجرور)	اثني عشر طالبا	اثنتي عشرة طالبة

Numbers 13–19:

The counted noun التمييز and the numeral are always accusative منصوب.
As to gender agreement, the first element disagrees in gender with the
noun التمييز while the second element agrees.

ثلاثة عشر طالبا	ثلاث عشرة طالبة
أربعة عشر طالبا	أربع عشرة طالبة
خمسة عشر طالبا	خمس عشرة طالبة
ستة عشر طالبا	ست عشرة طالبة
سبعة عشر طالبا	سبع عشرة طالبة
ثمانية عشر طالبا	ثمان عشرة طالبة
تسعة عشر طالبا	تسع عشرة طالبة

Numbers 20–99:

The noun التمييز is always accusative منصوب. In 20, 30, . . . etc. the same
form is used with any case or gender. For the first element (the unit number),
the above mentioned rules (3–10) must be applied as to case and gender.

عشرون طالبا	عشرون طالبة
أحد وعشرون طالبا	إحدى وعشرون طالبة
اثنان وعشرون طالبا	اثنتان وعشرون طالبة
خمسة وعشرون طالبا	خمس وعشرون طالبة
ثلاثون طالبا	ثلاثون طالبة
تسعون طالبا	تسعون طالبة

Hundreds and thousands:

The numeral and the counted noun form an *idaafa* construction. The
counted noun التمييز is always genitive مجرور for being مضاف إليه.

	مائة طالب	مائة طالبة
(مرفوع)	مائتا طالب	مائتا طالبة
(منصوب ـ مجرور)	مائتي طالب	مائتي طالبة
	ثلاث مائة طالب	ثلاث مائة طالبة
	ألف طالب	ألف طالبة
	ثلاثة آلاف طالب	ثلاثة آلاف طالبة
	عشرون ألف طالب	عشرون ألف طالبة

اسم التفضيل
Comparatives and Superlatives

1. اسم التفضيل is a derived noun indicating that two objects have something in common but one of them has more of the trait described than the other.

2. For form I verbs, اسم التفضيل is formed according to the pattern أفعل. For example:

أكبر - أجمل - أطول - أحدث

3. For forms other than form I verbs, اسم التفضيل is formed by placing the verbal noun after the pattern أفعل of a three radical verb suitable in meaning. For example:

أكثر - أشد - أحسن

السعودية من أكثر دول العالم إنتاجًا للنفط .

4. As a comparative adjective, اسم التفضيل is always masculine, singular, and indefinite.

5. The object to be compared is introduced by the preposition من. For example:

سلاح الغذاء أقوى من سلاح القنبلة الذرية .

6. When اسم التفضيل is definite (having the definite article or being the first term of an *idaafa*) it indicates the highest degree or the superlative meaning. For example:

سلاح الغذاء هو الأقوى . — سلاح الغذاء أقوى الأسلحة .

المستثنى

Exceptions

1. المستثنى is an accusative noun that comes after إلّا (أداة استثناء), with the condition that the exceptive proposition includes مستثنى منه and is affirmative.

حضر الطلاب إلا واحدا.

2. The exceptive proposition جملة الاستثناء consists of:

المستثنى منه   (الطلاب)
أداة الاستثناء   (إلا)
المستثنى   (واحدا)

3. If the proposition is negated, المستثنى may be either accusative منصوب or marked according to its grammatical function in the sentence يعرب بحسب موقعه في الجملة. Examples:

لم يحضر الطلابُ إلا واحدا. (مستثنى منصوب)
لم يحضر الطلابُ إلا واحدٌ. (بدل مرفوع)

4. When the exceptive proposition is negated and المستثنى منه is not clearly stated, then المستثنى is marked according to its grammatical function يعرب بحسب موقعه في الجملة. Examples:

لم يحضر إلا واحدٌ. (فاعل)
لم أقرأ إلا كتاباً. (مفعول به)

5. There are other particles: غير - سوى — خلا - عدا - حاشا

6. المستثنى after سوى - غير as مجرور is always in the genitive case مضاف إليه. For example:

لم يحضر سوى <u>طالبٍ</u>.

7. After حاشا - عدا - خلا, المستثنى may b accusative or genitive منصوب أو مجرور. For example:

حضر الطلاب عدا <u>واحداً</u>. (مفعول به)
حضر الطلاب عدا <u>واحدٍ</u>. (اسم مجرور بحرف جر)

8. خلا - عدا may be preceded by ما. In this case, المستثنى must be accusative for being مفعول به. For example:

حضر الطلاب ما عدا <u>واحداً</u>.

1. المنادى is a noun that follows one of the vocative particles which should be used when someone is directly addressed by name or title.

يا أحمد - يا أستاذ أحمد

2. أدوات النداء (vocative particles) are: يا - أ - أيا - هيا - أي. The most frequently used in Modern Standard Arabic is يا.

3. المنادى is منصوب (accusative) if it is:

   a. إضافة (idaafa): يا عبدَ الله - يا مدرسَ الفصلِ

   b. نكرة غير مقصودة (no specific person is addressed): يا رجلا.

4. المنادى is مرفوع (nominative) and without تنوين if it is:

   a. علم (proper noun): يا أحمدُ

   b. نكرة مقصودة (a specific person is addressed): يا طلابُ

5. If a common noun with the definite article is addressed:

   a. the particles أيها (مذكر) - أيتها (مؤنث) are used after the vocative particle يا.

   b. or a suitable demonstrative is used.

يا هذه الطالبة. — يا هؤلاء الطلاب.

6. The vocative particle may be deleted.

أحمد. — سيداتي وسادتي.

أسلوب التعجب
Wonder Construction

1. It is a construction used to express wonder or surprise.

ما أجمل الفتاة! (How beautiful the girl is.)

ما: اسم نكرة في محل رفع مبتدأ
أجمل: فعل ماض - الفاعل ضمير مستتر وجوبا تقديره هو
الفتاة: مفعول به منصوب بالفتحة
والجملة الفعلية في محل رفع خبر

Examples:

ما أجملَ الخطَ العربيّ! (How beautiful Arabic calligraphy is.)
ما أسهلَ هذا الدرس! (How easy this lesson is.)
ما أجملَها! (How beautiful she is.)

2. It consists of three basic elements:

a. ما التعجبيّة (Particle of wonder)

b. فعل التعجب (Verb of wonder) which is derived from an adjective according to the pattern أفعل

c. المتعجب منه (Object that causes wonder), which is an accusative noun (اسم منصوب) or a pronoun (ضمير).

ما أسهل الدرسَ! - ما أسهلهُ!

3. In order to use this pattern, the verb must be:

- a three-radical verb (فعل ثلاثي).

- a complete verb (not كان for example).
- affirmative (مُثْبَتا).
- active (مبنيا للمعلوم).
- fully inflected (ماض - مضارع - أمر).

And the adjective derived from it is not formed according to the pattern (أفعل - فعلاء).

4. Wonder or surprise can be also expressed by the pattern (أَفْعِلْ بـ). This pattern is rare in the Modern Standard Arabic. For example:

أجمل بالفتاة!

5. Wonder or surprise can be also expressed with some expressions like:

يا لَهَا من فتاة جميلة! - يا لَجمال الفتاة!

If the conditions mentioned in No. 3 are not fulfilled, wonder is expressed by using a helping verb plus the verbal noun المصدر الصريح أو المصدر المؤول as follows:

- ما أجمل أن نسافر في رحلة / السفر في رحلة! (فعل غير ثلاثي)
- ما أشد سواد الليل! (الوصف على وزن أفعل فعلاء)
- ما أصعب ألا ننجح! (الفعل منفي)
- ما أعظم أن يقال الحق! / ما أعظم قول الحق! (الفعل مبني للمجهول)

لا النافية للجنس
Absolute Negation

1. لا introduces nominal sentences for absolute negation.

2. After لا, المبتدأ (the subject) is مبني على الفتح (Which means that it does not take *tanween*), and it is called اسم لا.

لا دخانَ بدون نار.
لا حولَ ولا قوة إلا بالله.

3. The difference between لا and ليس is:

لا دخان بدون نار. (There is no smoke [absolutely] withoutfire.)
ليس الدخان بدون نار. (The smoke is not without fire.)

4. It is considered زائدة and so it does not affect the case of the subject if:
   a. The subject is definite. In this case, it must be repeated.

لا أحمد ولا علي.
   b. It is preceded by a preposition. أجبت بلا تفكير.
   c. Anything separates it from its noun.

الفيلم ممل، لا فيه تسلية ولا معلومات.

5. In some cases the predicate is omitted if it is understood from the context.

لا شك. (في كلامك)

جملة الشرط
Conditional Sentence

1. The conditional sentence consists of three main parts:
   - Conditional particle (أداة الشرط).
   - Condition clause (فعل الشرط).
   - Result clause (جواب الشرط) which states the consequences of the condition clause.

2. If the result clause does not begin with the perfect (فعل ماض) or jussive (فعل مضارع مجزوم), it is usually introduced by ـفَ.

3. Arabic has three conditional particles أدوات شرط translatable to English by 'if.' However, differences in their meanings are:

   a. (إذا) implies some degree of probability or reality in the present or future.
   - It is always followed by a perfect tense verb فعل ماض regardless of whether present, or future time is involved. For example:

   إذا ذاكر نجح. (If he studies, he will succeed.)

   إذا ذاكر فسينجح. (If he studies, he will succeed.)

   - As noted from the previous example, if the verb in جواب الشرط is not in the perfect tense, then جواب الشرط must be introduced by ـفَ.

   - If a nominal sentence is to be put as فعل الشرط , an appropriate form of the perfect tense of (كان) must be inserted after the particle.

For example: إذا كنت مخلصا فساعدنا. (If you are sincere, help us.)

b. (إنْ) is a straight hypothesis (if it is the case that).

- introduces a purely hypothetical condition, with no implication of degree of probability of fulfillment or non-fulfillment.

- The verb after it may be jussive (مجزوم) or perfect (ماض) with no change in meaning. In the case of being مجزوم, the verb in جواب الشرط cannot be perfect (ماض). For example:

إن ذاكرَ نجحَ. - إن يذاكرْ ينجحْ. (If he should study he will succeed.)

- If the verb in جواب الشرط is not perfect (ماض) or jussive (مضارع) جواب الشرط must be introduced by ـف, so جواب الشرط (مجزوم). Examples:

إن يذاكر فسوف ينجح. (If he studies he will succeed.)

إن يذاكر فقد ينجح. (If he studies he may succeed.)

c. (لو) deals with an imaginary or improbable situation which is unlikely to happen (contrary to fact).

- It is always followed by a perfect tense verb (فعل ماض). For example:

لو درس لنجح. (If he had studied he would have succeeded.)

- If a nominal sentence is to be put as فعل الشرط, an appropriate form of the perfect tense of (كان) is to be inserted after the particle. Examples:

لو كنت مكانك لفعلت ذلك. (If I were you I would do that *or* I would have done that.)

لو كنت مكانك لما/ما فعلت ذلك. (If I were you I would not do that *or* I would not have done that.)

- ـلَ must introduce جواب الشرط when it is ماض.

- If the verb in جواب الشرط is negated (ما + ماضي) must be used. In this case, the use of لَ is optional.

4. There are other particles, such as:

a. (لولا) means (if not, but for)

- It is always followed by a noun. Examples:

لولا صديقي لكنت وحيدا. (But for my friend I would be lonely.)

لولا صديقي لما/ما كنت وحيدا. (But for my friend I would not be lonely.)

- As noted from the previous example, جواب الشرط is to be introduced by لَ when it is affirmative, while the use of لَ is optional when it is negated by ما.

- The verb in جواب الشرط is always in the perfect tense (ماض).

b. There are other particles that can be followed by فعل ماض or مضارع مجزوم such as:

- أينما - حيثما (where, wherever). For example:

أينما تذهبْ نذهبْ. - أينما ذهبتَ ذهبنَا. (Wherever you go we will go.)

- مهما (whatever, no matter what). For example:

مهما تفعلْ فلن أغضبْ. (Whatever you do, I will not be angry.)

- من (who). For example: من يقرأ كثيراً يتعلمْ كثيرا.

- ما (what). For example: ما تقرأ يفدْك كثيرا.

5. In some cases the order of the parts of أسلوب الشرط is reversed, and جواب الشرط comes first. In this case ف is not used. For example:

سوف ينجح إذا ذاكر. - إذا ذاكر فسوف ينجح.

الجملة التي لها محل من الإعراب
Sentences That Function as Words

الإعراب	مثال	الموقع من الإعراب
يدرس: فعل مضارع مرفوع الفاعل ضمير مستتر تقديره هو العربية: مفعول به منصوب بالفتحة <u>والجملة في محل رفع خبر</u>	الطالب <u>يدرس العربية</u>.	١. خبر جملة اسمية
يدرس: فعل مضارع مرفوع الفاعل ضمير مستتر تقديره هو <u>والجملة في محل نصب خبر كان</u>	كان الطالب <u>يدرس</u>.	٢. خبر كان
يدرس: فعل مضارع مرفوع الفاعل ضمير مستتر تقديره هو الطب: مفعول به منصوب بالفتحة <u>الجملة في محل رفع خبر إن</u>	إن ابني <u>يدرس الطب</u>.	٣. خبر إن
سـ: حرف استقبال أدرس: فعل مضارع مرفوع الفاعل ضمير مستتر تقديره أنا العربية: مفعول به منصوب بالفتحة <u>والجملة في محل نصب مفعول به</u>	قال: <u>سأدرس العربية</u>.	٤. مفعول به لقال

الموقع من الإعراب	مثال	الإعراب
٥. حال	دخل الطالب الفصل وفي يده كتاب.	في: حرف جر يده: يد اسم مجرور بعد في وعلامة جره الكسرة والهاء: ضمير مبني في محل جر مضاف إليه والجار والمجرور في محل رفع خبر مقدم كتاب: مبتدأ مؤخر مرفوع بالضمة الجملة الاسمية في محل نصب حال
٦. صفة	دخل طالب يضحك.	يضحك: فعل مضارع منصوب والفاعل ضمير مستتر تقديره هو والجملة في محل رفع صفة
٧. مضاف إليه	جلست حيث يجلس أصدقائي.	يجلس: فعل مضارع مرفوع أصدقائي: أصدقاء فاعل مرفوع بالضمة، والضمير في محل جر مضاف إليه والجملة في محل جر مضاف إليه
٨. جواب لشرط جازم	من جد فالنجاح مؤكد.	النجاح: مبتدأ مرفوع بالضمة مؤكد: خبر مرفوع بالضمة والجملة في محل جزم جواب الشرط

الإعراب	مثال	الموقع من الإعراب
معه: مع حرف جر والهاء ضمير في محل جر، والجار والمجرور في محل رفع خبر مقدم حقيبة: مبتدأ مؤخر مرفوع بالضمة <u>والجملة في محل نصب جملة تابعة لجملة في محل نصب</u>	دخل الطالب وفي يده كتاب <u>ومعه حقيبة.</u>	٩. تابعة لجملة لها محل من الإعراب

أنواع (لا)
Types of *Laa*

مثال	تأثيرها على الإعراب	نوع (لا)
لا نفهمُ الدرس.	لا تؤثر	١. حرف نفي تدخل على الفعل المضارع
لا تنمْ في الفصل.	تجزم الفعل	٢. حرف جزم (لا الناهية) تدخل على الفعل المضارع
أحب القهوة لا الشاي.	ما بعدها يعرب كما قبلها	٣. حرف عطف تدخل على الاسم
لا إلهَ إلا الله.	المبتدأ يبنى على ما ينصب به	٤. لا النافية للجنس تدخل على الاسم
لا طالبَ موجودا.	تنصب الخبر	٥. لا نافية من أخوات ليس تدخل على الجملة الاسمية بشرط أن يكون المبتدأ والخبر نكرتين
لا الطالبُ ولا الأستاذُ في الفصل. سأدرس القواعد بلا ترددٍ.	لا تؤثر	٦. حرف نفي زائد تدخل على اسم معرفة أو يسبقها حرف جر

أنواع (ما)
Types of *Maa*

مثال	تأثيرها على الإعراب	نوع (ما)
أعجبني كل ما قرأت. (ما: اسم موصول مبني في محل جر مضاف إليه)	اسم وتعرب حسب موقعها في الجملة	١. ما الموصولة
ما اسمك؟ (ما: اسم مبني في محل رفع خبر)	اسم يعرب حسب موقعه في الجملة	٢. ما الاستفهامية
ما أجمل الطبيعة. (ما: اسم نكرة مبن في محل رفع مبتدأ)	اسم وتعرب مبتدأ	٣. ما التعجبية
ما تقرأ يفدك.	اسم شرط يجزم فعلين	٤. ما الشرطية
ما حضر الطالب.	حرف ينفي الفعل، خصوصا الماضي ولا تؤثر على الإعراب	٥. ما نافية للفعل
ما الدرس صعبا. ما الدنيا إلا مسرح كبير.	حرف نفي ينصب الخبر إذا أضيفت (إلا) قبل الخبر، فلا تؤثر ما على الإعراب	٦. ما نافية (من أخوات ليس)
إنما الناس متساوون. (إن الناس متساوين)	حرف يتصل بإن ويمنع عمل إن	٧. ما زائدة كافة عن العمل

نوع (ما)	تأثيرها على الإعراب	مثال
8. ما زائدة غير كافة عن العمل	حرف يتصل بحروف الجر ولا يؤثر على الإعراب	عما قليل (عن: حرف جر - ما زائدة - قليل: اسم مجرور بالكسرة)

43

أنواع حتى
Types of *Hatta*

The types of حتى are:

1. A preposition حرف جر which introduces nouns, and the noun after it is in the genitive case مجرور. It means 'until.' For example:

قرأت الكتاب حتى آخره. (I read the book till its end.)

2. حرف نصب which introduces verbs and change their mood from indicative الرفع to subjunctive النصب. It means 'in order to' (لـ - كي - لكي). For example:

ذاكرت كثيرا حتى تنجحَ. (She studied hard in order to succeed.)

3. A conjunction حرف عطف which means 'even' and the noun after it follows the case of the noun before it. For example:

يحب الناسُ كرة القدم حتى الأطفالُ. (People like football, even children.)

4. An inceptive حرف ابتداء which introduces a new sentence. It may mean 'so that.' For example:

ذاكرت جيدا حتى إنني أفهم الدروس تماما.

(I studied hard so that I now understand the lessons well.)